'If ever a book could ch[...]
excuses for wringing [...]
while the planet dies. In [...]
Lisa Harrow has given [...]
Get out there and use it.[...]
Nicholas Evans

'I have seen the dying coral in the South Pacific, in the Caribbean and in the Sea of Cortez. I have tasted the smog in Los Angeles and Manila, and I have seen buildings crumbling into the streets rotted by pollution in Mexico City. I have witnessed the monumental waste of resources all over the world, and the governments' inertia or simple indifference. Now Lisa Harrow has given us a handbook to help each of us make a personal start on doing our bit to preserve the planet for future generations.'
Patrick Stewart

'This little book could change your life. Read it and use it and give it to anyone who is a parent, a grandparent, an aunt or uncle or citizen of the world who believes that we should leave the world as we had the luck to find it. This earth is not ours, it is merely lent to us for our lifetimes, and this book shows us how we may return it well looked after, rather than abused. This little book inspires, educates and empowers.'
Helena Bonham Carter

'Lisa Harrow has written a comprehensive and annotated guide to websites oriented to useful, local activities that you can take to help create a sustainable future. It is introduced by her husband Roger Payne, who is the co-discoverer of whale song and one of my heroes. It is a remarkable little book. Buy it. And use it.'
Professor Lord Robert May, Oxford University

What Can I Do? is a joy. May it be kept handy by all who need a quick, useful answer to the question posed in the title.'
E. O. Wilson

Lisa Harrow, a New Zealander by birth, joined the Royal Shakespeare Company in 1969 and played leading roles in many of their productions, including Olivia in *Twelfth Night*, Desdemona in *Othello*, Portia in *Merchant of Venice* and Lady Amaranth in *Wild Oats*. She also played Ann Whitfield in *Man and Superman* opposite Peter O'Toole on a national tour and in the West End.

She starred in TV shows such as the BBC series *Nancy Astor*, *Sense of Guilt*, and *Kavanagh QC*.

Lisa made her New York début playing Vivian Bearing in the acclaimed off-Broadway production of *Wit*. Other work in America has included productions of *Medea*, *Copenhagen*, *All My Sons* and *Mary Stuart*.

She won the Australian Oscar for Best Actress for *The Last Days of Chez Nous*, and the film *Sunday* won the Grand Jury Award at the 1997 Sundance Film Festival and earned Lisa a nomination for an Independent Spirit Award for Best Actress.

Lisa now lives in Vermont with her husband, whale biologist Roger Payne, and her son Timothy.

For further information you can go to **whatcanidousa.org**. If you have any web addresses, information or updates that could be included in the next edition of *What Can I Do?* please email them to **lisa@whatcanidousa.org**.

WHAT CAN I DO?

The A–Z guide to eco-friendly internet
sites, ideas and information in the UK

Lisa Harrow

eden project **books**

TRANSWORLD PUBLISHERS
61–63 Uxbridge Road, London W5 5SA
a division of The Random House Group Ltd
www.booksattransworld.co.uk

First published in Great Britain in 2007 by Eden Project Books
a division of Transworld Publishers

A CIP catalogue record for this book
is available from the British Library.

ISBN 9781905811045

Addresses for Random House Group Ltd companies outside the
UK can be found at: www.randomhouse.co.uk
The Random House Group Ltd Reg. No. 954009

Typeset in 9/12pt Din by
Falcon Oast Graphic Art Ltd.

Printed and bound in Great Britain by
Cox & Wyman Ltd, Reading, Berkshire.

2 4 6 8 10 9 7 5 3 1

Mixed Sources

Product group from well-managed
forests and other controlled sources
www.fsc.org Cert no. TT-COC-2139
© 1996 Forest Stewardship Council

For my father, Ken Harrow, who planted the seed.

For my husband, Roger Payne, who nurtured its growth.

For my son, Tim Harrow, who will reap the harvest.

CONTENTS

D

E

F

G

M

N

O

P

Q

W

X

Y

Z

LISA'S PREFACE

25 May 1991 was a beautiful day in London, with an uncharacteristically clear blue sky. Looking back, my eight-year-old son Tim and I, if we were at all superstitious, might have taken such a beautiful day as a sign that our lives were about to change. For ever. But that kind of prescience only happens in fairy tales. The reality of our day was that we were heading to a 'Save the Whales' rally in Trafalgar Square – something we'd never done before. Greenpeace had asked me to be a 'celebrity speaker', to read a piece about how some whales communicate across thousands of miles of deep ocean with sounds that can also travel through the mantle of the Earth. That astonished me. Even though I had grown up in New Zealand, where whales were once abundant, I knew nothing about these mysterious animals. The only whale I'd ever seen had been lying dead on the beach.

We stood at the back of a large crowd and watched the opening speech, delivered by one Roger Payne, heralded as the co-discoverer of humpback-whale song. That too was a surprise to me. I'd never heard of such a thing. He was an impassioned speaker, but I was much more focused on my nerves than on what he was saying. This was the first time I had ever addressed a large crowd without the carapace of a play, a character and weeks of rehearsal to protect me.

Roger was at the foot of the stairs when I finished my piece. 'Have you ever seen a whale from close quarters?' The voice was warm and humorous, matching the eyes. I said I hadn't, and as we talked, we began making plans to do so in the coming summer, and I found myself thinking of all the adventures Tim and I could share with this extraordinarily charming man who was so full of amazing stories. My complex life as a working actress and single mother suddenly seemed so simple. Three hours later we were still talking. Ten weeks later we were married.

Meeting Roger was transformational. As we stood there exchanging words and ideas, enfolding large chunks of our lives into passionate abbreviations – as one does upon instantly falling in love with someone – I felt as if I were at the edge of an ocean, ankle-deep in the incoming waves, staring out at the vast expanse of sunlit possibilities.

We were married in Woodstock, Vermont that summer and the adventures began. Tim and I started spending time with whales and experiencing their awesome size and sheer beauty. Off the coast of California we watched dolphins riding on the bow waves of incomprehensibly huge blue whales. At Peninsula Valdez in Argentina we were lulled to sleep by the sound of right whales breathing in the bay. In Alaska the piercing cries of humpbacks echoed through our boat as they corralled fish in their nets made from bubbles, and we watched amazed as they erupted out of the depths, mouths gaping wide to engulf the 'netted' fish. Sitting in a small open boat in Laguna San Ignacio, we stroked the head of a grey whale that came alongside for a visit. With the adventures came a growing understanding of Roger's world, and through that understanding, a gradual awakening to the environmental problems Earth faces.

We learned that everything in Nature is connected. Human beings are not separate from the rest of life on Earth, but an integral part of it. Thus everything we do has consequences: seemingly pristine lakes in the far north contain fish that are heavily polluted with industrial chemicals produced thousands of miles away, deposited there by circulating air currents. The relentless development of new ways to harvest more and more fish from the ocean is resulting in fewer and fewer fish to catch. The pursuit of cheap food is destroying soils and wildlife, and filling our bodies with toxins that disrupt hormones and diminish the ability of our children to learn. Access to fresh water is becoming a serious problem worldwide.

Three years ago, Roger conceived the idea of Lessons from Copernicus (Now called SeaChange: Reversing the Tide), a performance piece involving us both, which used science and poetry to highlight both the problems we face, and the exciting solutions that humanity is inventing to solve those problems. After our first performance I saw that many of the audience were overwhelmed by the enormity of the environmental stresses we had highlighted. It was clear they wanted to do something, but didn't know where to start. I realized we needed to give them a tool to help them gain a deeper understanding about what was going wrong, and what they could do to become part of the solution. So I put together a booklet full of useful Internet sites, to be given away free to everyone who came to the performance.

That first little book was picked up, expanded and published by Chelsea Green in the USA, and since then I have produced two separate editions for Australia and New Zealand, and now this one for the UK. I hope it finds a home by your computer. The Internet is one of humanity's greatest inventions. Through it we have easy access to the information we need to make good decisions about how to live. It can join us together in common causes, and empowered by that connection, we can have the greatest possible impact as we fight together for those causes.

For years I had gone about my life, aware somewhere on the periphery of my concerns that fish were becoming a scarce resource, that the rainforests were being destroyed, that modern agricultural and industrial practices were debilitating our world and us. But I had not really paid much attention. Life with Roger changed my focus. I began to think about the consequences of my actions. I began to change the way I lived. I recycled. I filled our house with compact fluorescent bulbs and energy-efficient machines. I bought a hybrid car. I became aware of what we were eating and how it had arrived on our plates. I became passionate about the possibility of transforming lakes of manure into electricity, thus solving the awful problems of groundwater pollution and the appalling smell created by such manure lagoons. I began to carry around lists of which fish are sustainably harvested and healthy to eat, and to share those lists with my friends and the waiters in restaurants. I started noticing wind farms wherever I was in the world, marvelling at their silent beauty and at all the clean electricity they were producing. I started buying plastic bags made from corn. And most of all, I began to get very assertive about not wasting water.

Changing the way we live requires that we first understand what the problems are, how they are caused, and how to solve them. This book will introduce you to simple but revolutionary choices that can profoundly affect your health and the health of the rest of life on Earth. If we follow the laws of Nature when producing energy, dealing with waste, growing food and manufacturing things, the destruction will stop. Life on Earth will continue into an unimagined future where, generations hence, our children's children will bless us and thank us for our heedfulness. And we can be proud that we are part of the twenty-first-century revolution, where ordinary people are dreaming of, demanding, and achieving solutions beyond anything previously thought possible.

ROGER PAYNE'S INTRODUCTION

....

When I met Lisa Harrow at that Greenpeace rally, I fell in love with her in the first forty-five seconds, maybe less. When she was speaking, I couldn't see her from where I was standing, but the intelligence of her voice came burning through all the traffic and hubbub of Trafalgar Square. As he thanked Lisa, the host of the rally said, 'I wish all of you could see Miss Harrow's blue eyes up close. She has such beautiful eyes.' He was dead right. But I think it was her fierce intelligence that stole my heart entirely. As we talked, I quickly established that she was neither married nor involved with anyone else. All I could think of was, 'How can I marry this extraordinary creature?'

I was staying with a friend in London who knew Lisa's work from television, and that night, when I told him that I had met her and was determined to marry her, he turned to his partner and murmured, 'In his dreams.'

At the moment I met Lisa, her son Tim was off with his nanny, playing on Trafalgar Square's famous bronze lions. When he appeared, half an hour later, I had already realized that unless Tim approved, a relationship with Lisa would never work. So I determined there and then that Tim should never feel left out of anything we did. Thus our first date, the following morning, was a trip to London Zoo with Tim, his nanny and two cousins. Two weeks later, Lisa had agreed to marry me.

But I felt that I must ask Tim for her hand, and that if he didn't approve we shouldn't go through with it. He was in

London; I was now in Boston. It was the scariest phone call I've ever made. But when I blurted out my request, he calmly said, 'Yes,' and then, with a dignity that only an extraordinary eight-year-old can achieve, added, 'This is the happiest day of my life.' Heaven knows, it was mine.

I could work from anywhere with a phone and a laptop, so after we were married I moved to London and started accompanying Lisa wherever her work took her. When she did a play I'd try to see all the performances (I watched her do *Wit* forty-two times), and from this I began to appreciate more fully what a remarkable ability she possessed. She could speak not just to someone's reasoning mind, but to their soul, and it occurred to me that if it were possible to focus the burning glass of that ability on the problems humanity has created for life on Earth, she might start bigger waves through the human psyche than any mere scientist could ever achieve. It was with that in mind that I set out to write *Lessons from Copernicus* – a programme we could do together, and which, after many rewrites, is now called *SeaChange: Reversing the Tide*.

Its message is about the importance of our species living in accordance with the laws of Nature – living life sustainably by obeying natural laws. One of the most appealing reasons for embracing such a major lifestyle change is the sheer delight of the vistas that open up to anyone who makes their way along the road to sustainability, while learning to live in the world without destroying it. It also transforms our current landscape of despair into one of hope.

As Lisa and I researched our programme, we gained an exciting, unexpected and hopeful insight: that humanity's worst problems are *solvable*; that most solutions are *simple*; and that existing scientific knowledge is *sufficient* to get on with the solutions. It became clear that current science provides enough understanding for us to act; it is the collective will of humanity that needs work. And what might Lisa and I do to help fortify that will? Such fortification has occurred before, when dissatisfaction with the status quo has roused people to action, and the success of their actions has energized them enough to achieve true changes. It always seems to have been a process involving both information and inspiration. Perhaps Lisa and I could engage listeners by combining the inspiration of art and poetry with the information of science – thereby engaging both sides of people's brains at the same time.

I had started from a sense of hopelessness, but our first effort at this dual approach convinced me that it might just work. In any case, we could both see that what we were doing lay on a path towards hope, where small nudges can unleash cascades of beneficial change. We began to realize that millions of people are awaiting a movement to join, and that when it appears they will recognize it and unite their actions to achieve change.

And what is at stake? No generation that has come before us has ever had such a huge opportunity for greatness, simply because never before have the stakes been so high. But that also means that if you and I fail to act, ours will become the most vilified generation in human history. The youth of the future will despise us simply because we couldn't muster the will to change our ways, even though we understood the dire consequences of our inaction. Our descendants will see that clearly.

But if we act, we will be honoured as the greatest of generations, and will redefine the words 'hero' and 'heroine'. And our descendants will boast of us as of kings and queens.

A

ACTION

Everything in this book is aimed at encouraging us to look at the way we live and how we might change it to embrace a more environmentally friendly lifestyle. The following organizations are on the frontline of such change.

www.campaigncc.org

An impressive list of people, led by the indomitable George Monbiot, heads the Campaign against Climate Change, which has been established to fight the 'ignorance, inertia, short-term greed and vested interests' that are preventing the cessation of the immense damage that climate change is inflicting upon the Earth. The group wants you to add your voice to the thousands that are fighting to reverse the political will of governments and corporate leaders worldwide. **Find your local group** and join the action.

www.ciwf.org.uk

Compassion in World Farming's mission is to advance the well-being of farm animals worldwide, and they have been investigating, campaigning and lobbying since 1967 on behalf of those animals. CIWF **campaigns** in several arenas – the suffering of animals during long-distance transport, the care of poultry, and why it's important to eat less meat. **Get involved** has a number of suggestions, from choosing free-range or organic meat and eggs to becoming a 'compassionate campaigner'.

www.cpre.org.uk
The Campaign to Protect Rural England believes that a sustainably maintained and productive rural landscape is beneficial to all, and since 1926 that has been their mission, in both local and national arenas. If you are interested in joining the action, **campaigns** lists the causes. If you are concerned that overdevelopment is degrading your environment, **planninghelp** has the tools to help you influence how that new development progresses.

www.doingyourbit.org.uk
If you do nothing else, print out this list, attach it to your fridge and the noticeboard at work, and follow these suggestions. Before you know it, you will be on the path to a sustainable way of life.

www.eia-international.org
The Environmental Investigation Agency is an undercover agency working to stop environmental crime. The collection of scrupulous scientific documentation is their tool, and that evidence has been used successfully at international conventions to affect public policy. **Latest news** will enable you to catch up on what's happening with their **campaigns**. Images from those campaigns are available in **visual media**.

www.foe.co.uk
Friends of the Earth: tried and true, like all real friends. These friends fight tirelessly for the betterment of life on Earth. Join them and become part of this massive global network of people steadily working for a fairer, cleaner, more stable and healthier world. Climate change, corporate responsibility for environmental degradation,

protection of the world's biodiversity, reduction of waste through recycling, and the promotion of healthy, non-GMO food are just some of the myriad of issues about which this site has excellent information. Sign up on **campaign express**, and start to actively make a change.

www.globalactionplan.org.uk

Global Action Plan offers practical advice for positive change. For basic information explore **your environment**, and then use the links to help you decide where to begin. **Energy bike** presents an interesting connection between pedalling and leaving the TV on standby, or boiling the kettle. **At work** offers support to companies wanting to save money by cutting waste and energy consumption. If you and your neighbours want to start living more sustainably, **EcoTeams** in **schools and community** has the blueprint.

www.greenpeace.org.uk

Greenpeace is an independent organization that has used non-violent, direct action to create a healthier, more humane world since the 1970s. If you want to stop nuclear war, clean up the oceans, save endangered species, encourage the spread of food that is wholesome and nourishing, work to change energy policies to halt climate change, save some of the most ancient forest areas in the world, lobby to remove toxins from our life and ensure the well-being of future generations, this site is a wonderful place to start.

www.passport.panda.org

Environmental activism from your desktop. Register for **your passport** and join the **campaigns** for action organized by WWF to help with environmental problems worldwide. Passport-holders have had many victories, including a recent one in New Zealand waters, when they ensured the protection of the critically endangered Maui dolphin by calling for a ban on set nets in the inshore waters off the west coast of the North Island.

www.risingtide.org.uk

If the relentless progress of climate change is irksome to you, then join this grassroots coalition of groups and individuals who are building a movement to stop it. Click on **community** for contacts around the UK.

ARCHITECTURE

SEE ALSO: Building Green, Design, Eden Project, Natural Laws, Sustainable Living

www.arc-architects.co.uk

Arc is a Scottish company that specializes in sustainable architecture and the conservation of old buildings. **Affordable eco-house** in **architecture** shows their award-winning ecological house.

www.arco2.co.uk

This North Cornwall practice designs buildings that can include such sustainable techniques as green roofs, renewable energy sources, insulation made from recycled newspaper and sheep's wool, natural lighting, reed-bed drainage, grey-water recycling, straw-bale construction, and the use of FSC timbers. They build schools, gymnasiums, offices and multi-dwelling units, as well as conversions. **Portfolio** has pictures and fact sheets.

www.mcdonough.com

Visionary architect William McDonough (*Time* magazine's 1999 Hero of the Planet) is one of the prime movers behind the new industrial revolution, which is based on the implementation of natural laws throughout our design and industrial practices. On this site there are articles, films and the 'treeless' book *Cradle to Cradle*, which is in itself a revolution in design. Click on **www.mcdonoughpartners.com** for examples of his work for universities, zoos, sustainable communities in China, private homes, museums, and the Ford plant in Dearborn, Michigan, which has the largest green roof in the world.

www.zedfactory.com/home.html

ZedFactory introduces the exciting vision of Bill Dunster Architects. Here is the new carbon-neutral urban architecture, one that uses renewable energy, grey-water systems to recycle water and living machines for waste water, and has green roofs, support systems for families, and many other imaginative solutions for a comfortable, healthy way of life that will not cost the earth, but that will in fact replenish it. **BedZED**, an urban village, and the conference hall at **Earth Centre** already exist, and **Flower Tower, Hope House** and **Velocity** should do in the very near future. Living in cities has never been so much fun.

B

BATTERIES

SEE ALSO: Local Government, Mobile Phones, Reduce-Reuse-Recycle, Waste

The batteries used by modern portable technology release some appalling toxins when discarded or incinerated. Most contain heavy metals like mercury and cadmium that are now turning up in fish, which means that the fish may soon be unfit for human consumption. Rechargeable batteries are a better choice for the environment as they can be recharged several hundred times before they lose their efficacy. An even better choice are the new water-powered batteries, which you charge by refilling them with water.

www.apple.com.au/batteries
Tips on extending the battery life of your iPod, iBook or Powerbook.

www.tangogroup.co.uk
Click on **products**, and scroll down to the revolutionary water-powered batteries, which are non-toxic and recyclable. Use them for small electronic products like clocks and calculators. Get them here, or click on **stores** to see before you buy.

**www.wasteonline.org.uk/resources/InformationSheets/
Batteries.htm**
Waste Online's information sheet has the why, how, what
and where of battery recycling.

BICYCLES

SEE ALSO: London, National Parks, Sustainable Living

*With climate change on everyone's mind, and the price of
petrol on its inevitable upward climb, the humble bicycle is
back in vogue. Communities in Denmark, Norway, the US
and Canada have instituted bike-share schemes to
encourage people to leave the car at home. Perhaps this is
something you could organize in your town.*

www.atob.org.uk
If you're interested in buying an electric or folding bike, or
a bike trailer, you'll find everything you want to know
here.

www.bikeregister.com
Register your bike's details into a secure database, get it
tagged, and if it's stolen, then that information is available
to police nationwide.

www.ibike.org
The International Bicycle Fund offers a wealth of
resources for those interested in bicycling.
Encouragement and bike-to-work programmes opens
the door to ways in which we can begin to use bikes as a

sustainable way of getting about. Worldwide lists of community bike-share programmes, how to set up such a group in your neighbourhood, international bike adventures, an annual **essay contest** for young writers, safety, and urban planning for bikes are just a few of the topics covered on this site.

www.waterscape.com/cycling
Explore Britain's waterways on the many cycle paths available.

BIODIVERSITY

SEE ALSO: Conservation, Endangered Species, Environment

Every ecosystem requires a large number of species to maintain its health and stability. That means that every animal and plant must be stable and productive if life on Earth is to continue to flourish, as each is dependent on many others for its survival. According to DEFRA, 'In 2005 around 65 per cent of [non-marine] mammals and birds and 22 per cent of fish, amphibians and reptiles species assessed were considered "threatened" [and] just under a quarter of invertebrates and around a third of seed plants and ferns are threatened or nationally scarce.' Since the mid-1970s, populations of woodland and farmland birds such as the song thrush, starling and skylark have been in steady decline. Since the beginning of the last century over a hundred species in the UK have become extinct, and if we are not careful, other species and their habitats will follow. Biodiversity is essential to our well-being and we need to ensure its robust survival.

www.uksafari.com
Animals and nature has photographs and identifying information for many of the birds, insects, sea creatures, amphibians, spiders, trees, flowers, mammals, fungi and lichens with which we share the UK, and the **links** page is especially good.

www.wildfile.co.uk
The complex ecosystems that support life on Earth work best when all the species endemic to a particular ecosystem are given the opportunity to flourish. Wildfile has gathered a wide-ranging list of websites that deal with this issue. Unsung heroes of community endeavours are here, listed under **'unofficial' websites**. This huge site is one for a rainy day, and by the time the sun has returned, you will be amazed at the amount of work being carried forward by people to protect the biodiversity of the British Isles, and realize why it is essential to the future of our species.

BIRDS

....

SEE ALSO: Conservation, Endangered Species, Energy, Farming, Gardens, Keep UK Beautiful, National Parks, Reduce-Reuse-Recycle

....

www.barnowltrust.org.uk
The fact that the Barn Owl is one of the most studied birds in Britain is probably due in large degree to the work of the Barn Owl Trust. These beautiful birds used to be common, but since the 1930s their population has steadily declined. The Trust works for their **conservation** through **education** and **research**.

www.bto.org

Anyone interested in birds can be part of the data-collecting team of the British Trust for Ornithology, an independent organization that promotes the conservation of birds by the use of volunteer-based surveys. Click on **surveys** to get involved. Gardeners can join the **garden birdwatch** and there are **hot-weather tips** to help birds survive during droughts. If you enjoy watching birds, you could expand your circle of friends by joining in the **conferences and workshops**.

www.gigrin.co.uk

BBC *Wildlife Magazine* called the red kite-feeding station at Gigrin Farm in mid-Wales 'the largest, most fantastic bird table in the world'. Every day, you can see the spectacle as these glorious birds of prey jostle and compete with crows and buzzards for food. **Red-kite feeding station** has the details.

www.owls.org

Muncaster Castle in Cumbria is the home of the World Owl Trust, a charity that focuses on the conservation of owls and their habitat throughout the world. Visitors to the **World Owl Centre** can see over a hundred owls, from the biggest to some of the smallest. You can **meet the birds**, or if you really want get to know them, you can **volunteer** to clean out the cages, prepare their food or build their homes. For an other-worldly end to your visit, explore the **Meadow Vole Maze** beneath a wildflower meadow. **Habitat creation** encourages us to grow wildflowers on wasteground or in gardens to help the survival of all native species, including owls, and if you want to build a home for barn owls, there are nest-box designs to help you. **New owl species** has the latest news on recent discoveries.

www.rspb.org.uk

The Royal Society for the Protection of Birds pursues its goals through education, habitat conservation, policy initiatives, and the enforcement of environmental laws. Click on **birds** for the **A–Z of UK birds**, and **aren't birds brilliant!** for information on where to see birds in close proximity in the wild. **Visit our amazing reserves** introduces the many bird sanctuaries around the British Isles, and **follow our soap operas** are delightful webcam and written diaries of the daily activities in the nests of ospreys, eagles and peregrine falcons. There's a chance to put your **second-hand binoculars** to good use, and **advice** is full of ways for us to enjoy these beautiful and entertaining creatures.

www.wwt.org.uk

The Wildfowl and Wetlands Trust has **centres** throughout the UK, where visitors can see the birds and their habitats that have been protected by this charity since 1946. Click on the one nearest you and enjoy a day paddling about with the ducks, swans, geese and flamingos, as well as treasures like the rare avocets that hatched in the heart of the capital, at the **London Wetland Centre** in 2006. The WWT's conservation work is proving very successful – seven of their sites have been declared Sites of Special Scientific Interest (SSSIs) by English Nature.

BOOKS

Use your local library, and share or give away books you've read rather than throwing them away.

www.readitswapit.co.uk
An Internet book-exchange service that's free.

www.reuze.co.uk/books.shtml
Reuze offers a number of suggestions for places that will take donated books.

BUILDING GREEN

SEE ALSO: Architecture, Composting Toilets, Design, Eden Project, Energy, Home, Lighting, Natural Laws, Health, Reduce-Reuse-Recycle, Sustainable Living, Waste, Water

Sustainable building practices are becoming the norm as we learn more about how important they are to the health of our environment and ourselves.

www.ecopaints.com
Award-winning paints that are organic, odourless and solvent-free.

www.est.org.uk/housingbuildings/professionals
This site, hosted by the Energy Saving Trust, has technical guides and other information to help with designing and building energy-efficient homes, whether they are new or refurbished.

www.greenbuilder.co.uk
Everything you want to know about building green is here
– with information on self-building techniques, green
mortgages, architects and builders, specifications,
earthships (buildings made principally from used tyres
filled with earth), materials and much, much more.

www.greenregister.org
The Green Register is an online service where customers
can find builders committed to sustainable practices, and
where such builders can register. **Construction
professional** has details about **seminars and workshops**.

www.greenspec.co.uk
GreenSpec has information for all those in the
construction industry. Click on **background** and then
construction and the environment for a graphic
description as to why a sustainable construction process
is essential to the health of us all. **Products** has a huge
list of eco-friendly building materials and fittings, as well
as **reclaimed materials** for reuse. **Design** has **greener
specifications** and **links** will head you in the right
direction.

www.natural-building.co.uk
Natural Building Technologies evaluates the building
materials they sell in terms of their impact upon the
environment and human health, and whether they are
effective. For the ethos underlying the business, click on
ecology. To see where their products have been used,
click on **case studies**.

www.newbuilder.co.uk

The Green Building Press publishes information for all those interested in the construction of eco-friendly, healthy homes, offices and other buildings. The *Green Building Bible* offers comprehensive help in all the techniques necessary, plus information about grants for renewable-energy projects. Their magazine, *Building for a Future*, is the only one in the UK devoted to green building issues. **GreenPro** will give you access to green products, articles and information. The **forum** is open to all and covers a wide variety of personal experience with green building techniques. Those involved in the business of sustainable building should add their details to those already listed in **links**.

www.oldhousestore.co.uk

If you are renovating an old house, this seller of eco-friendly and traditional building materials might have just the old door handle you've been looking for. **Products** lists what's available. **Technical info** has practical guides on traditional and restorative building techniques.

www.sageoxford.org.uk/ecohouse.htm

On 16 June 2006, Averil Stedeford, a recently widowed grandmother, won the *Observer* Ethical Award for best DIY project, for the eco-retrofit of the dilapidated semi-detached house she had recently moved into in Headington, Oxford. You can follow the progress of the refit on this website, and perhaps be inspired to follow her example and do the same.

www.secondnatureuk.com

Thermafleece for insulating produced by a British company. **Case studies** has two examples of the material's effectiveness.

PEOPLE WHO DID

IF YOU SAW **Averil Stedeford** walking down the road, you wouldn't immediately think that she was a passionate environmentalist, yet at the age of seventy-three, she is pursuing a path that can only be seen in that light. Averil has become deeply concerned about the effect that climate change is having on our world, and she is determined to take steps to mitigate that effect for the sake of her grandchildren. Hence her decision to buy an ordinary semi-detached house in Headington, near Oxford, and turn it into a 'green' home. Averil made this decision after the death of her beloved husband, transforming her sense of loss into one of purpose, with the aim of achieving something that would give meaning to her grief.

Averil's belief that environmental healing starts at home has turned her into an expert on eco-refits. A huge tank that collects rainwater is buried in the back garden as part of a grey-water system to provide water for the laundry, the toilets and the garden. She has energy-efficient windows, photovoltaic cells on the roof for electricity and solar panels for heating water. She's become an expert on insulation, and is spreading that expertise around her neighbourhood. Her prize money from the *Observer* Ethical Award is being spent on a rooftop wind turbine; she is excited at the prospect of producing some of her own electricity, and is also hoping that her neighbours will follow her example and start installing windmills on their roofs. The last word should be left to the judges: 'Averil is an example to us all. When you look at how much she has achieved in her own home, anybody should be able to make radical changes, simple things that can lighten our environmental footprints on the Earth's resources.'

www.segalselfbuild.co.uk
The Walter Segal Self Build Trust promotes the benefits of communities building their own homes. Click on **recent highlights** and see what is possible if a community decides to get together and build, and then click on **resources** to get started.

www.sheepwoolinsulation.ie
Sheep's wool makes a non-toxic, efficient, re-usable and biodegradable insulation material and this Irish company sells it. **Thermal insulation** lists all the benefits. **Requirements** tells you how much you'll need, and if you want **acoustic insulation**, it works for that too.

www.sunpipe.co.uk/suncatcher/index.php
Cut down on air-conditioner use, save money and electricity, and reduce carbon emissions by installing Suncatcher, a single unit that will provide both natural ventilation and natural light.

BUSINESS

SEE ALSO: Cars, Climate Change, Energy, Golf, Investment, London, Meetings and Gatherings, Mobile Phones, Natural Laws, Office, Packaging, Paper, Reduce-Reuse-Recycle, Shopping Bags, Sustainable Living, Transportation, Waste, Worms

Businesses are learning that to be green means increased profits.

www.bestfootforward.com
Businesses and other organizations, as well as individuals, can put their best foot forward and use this group to

learn how to make their environmental footprint smaller by adopting more sustainable modes of operation.

www.bioregional.com/take_action/
take_action_bus.htm

Some guidelines for sustainable business practices from BioRegional, an enterprising and imaginative group that is bringing eco-friendly practices into the mainstream.

www.carbonneutral.com

The Carbon Neutral Company can help your business reduce the damaging carbon emissions that result from every aspect of your activity – the office, travel and production processes. They encourage the use of energy-efficient practices and renewables, in conjunction with the planting of forests to absorb the carbon dioxide already in the atmosphere, to help you achieve a carbon-neutral status. Click on **business benefits** to find out how this can benefit the profitability of your organization, as well as the Earth.

www.thecarbontrust.co.uk/energy

Practical advice to help businesses cut their energy costs.

www.epaw.co.uk

This resource-packed site offers invaluable help for those who want to introduce sustainable practices into their business, but aren't sure where to begin. **Environmental practice** is the place to start.

www.eta.co.uk/pages/business/57/default.htm

This site has many simple and practical ideas for ways in which businesses can lower the impact of company travel on the environment.

www.greenbiz.com

'The Resource Center on Business, the Environment and the Bottom Line' is an American site that is full of useful information applicable to businesses all over the world. It uses practical solutions and good-news stories to demonstrate that good environmental practices do benefit the bottom line. The **business toolbox** is packed with research, briefings, essentials and checklists.

www.greendragonems.com

Green Dragon is a Welsh consultancy with a five-step programme that helps companies develop a commitment to sound environmental practices in the workplace. **The standard** introduces the five necessary steps; **certified companies** lists the 754 organisations already committed; and there are **grants available.**

www.maximiseprofit.org.uk

Use these free government services to maximize your profit by minimizing your business waste. You will get workshops, seminars and advisory visits, as well as many online resources.

www.netregs.gov.uk

An online tool to guide small businesses through environmental regulations.

www.recyclite.co.uk

A recycler of fluorescent bulbs that deals in bulk numbers for businesses.

C

CARS

SEE ALSO: Action, Batteries, Climate Change, Films, London, Peak Oil, Tourism, Transportation, Wastes:Hazardous

Cars are among the worst polluters on the planet, yet we need them. Whenever possible, car-share or use public transport, and plan your daily activities to avoid unnecessary car trips. Consider hybrid technology for your next car, or one with low emissions and better mileage.

www.betterworldhandbook.com/gasoline.html
Social responsibility rankings for gas stations shows how 'green' your petrol provider is.

www.carpoolworld.com
Car-sharing worldwide.

www.carshare.com
A directory of car-sharing sites for the UK and the Republic of Ireland, offering a wide variety of choices to those interested in sharing the ride.

www.citycarclub.co.uk
You don't have to own a car if you live in a city. Join City Car Club, and then, if you need a car, pay by the hour for a car parked near you that you can use, then park and

leave. **Pricing** has the costs, and if you **own a car**, calculate how much you might save by using this service instead.

www.ecoinsurance.co.uk

Co-operative Insurance will offset 20 per cent of your car's CO_2 emissions as part of their service, and those driving a car from Tax Band A get a 10 per cent discount. They also make sure that their repairers recycle responsibly.

www.ecolane.co.uk

Use this site to find out about cleaner fuels, cleaner vehicles and ways of travel that do not destroy the environment. Click on **eBook** for the online *Green Buyer's Car Guide*.

www.goingreen.co.uk

Take a look at the UK's bestselling electric car. Buy a G-Wiz, and you'll be driving an emission-free, carbon-neutral, energy-efficient car, and you won't have to pay any road tax. If you live in London, you also get free parking and don't have to pay the congestion charge. This car saves you money, while you save the Earth. **Testimonials** will persuade you to immediately click on **test drive**.

www.liftshare.org

Log in as a new user, and find someone to share the ride, or a walking buddy, or cycling partner. **Business solutions** has lift-share schemes for schools, universities, hospitals, events, companies and local councils. **Transport** has links to many public-transport options.

www.prius.com

The world's most well-known hybrid car. Low emissions, low petrol costs and five-star safety.

www.share-a-lift.com

If you're employed in Staffordshire, this site run by the County Council will help you find someone to share the ride to work. **Scheme details** lists the benefits, registration information and how to connect with a ride companion.

www.stopurban4x4s.org.uk

This group is campaigning to remove big 4x4s from the urban streets, and the **reasons** why are clearly laid out in this site. Because these vehicles are considered by their owners to be safe, **safety** is a good place to start, and if that doesn't give you pause for thought, then **climate change** and **environment** might.

www.wikipedia.org/wiki/List_of_carfree_places

A worldwide list of car-free urban areas.

CHILDREN

SEE ALSO: Cleaning Products, Conscious Consumerism, Eden Project, Fish, Food, Food for Babies, Gifts, Health, Home, Nappies, Pesticides and Toxins, Plastic and Alternatives, Schools, Worms, Young People

www.checnet.org

The Children's Health Environmental Coalition is an information resource to help parents learn about the effect the toxic substances that surround us can have on their children, and what steps they can take to prevent those effects. Click on **protect your kids** to find out more.

www.ecocentric.co.uk

See **toys and stationery** for robust, recycled cardboard playhouses for children that can be decorated inside and out. And when the playhouse is ready for demolition, it can be recycled again.

www.lsx.org.uk/programmes/gsguide_page1224.aspx

The London Sustainability Exchange's free guide to green products and services for nurseries and childcare centres.

www.theorganicreport.org

The O'Mama Report is a great resource for mothers and others about organic agriculture and organic products. **Kitchen** has yummy recipes for children.

CLEANING PRODUCTS

SEE ALSO: Conscious Consumerism, Health, Home, Pesticides and Toxins, Vinegar

Many cleaning products contain petrochemical components that are harmful to people, animals and the environment. They degrade slowly, build up in the environment, and are toxic to aquatic life. Their production consumes large amounts of energy, reduces the world's diminishing supply of petroleum, and causes irreparable environmental damage during well-drilling and oil extraction. Use biodegradable cleaning products that don't contain harmful petrochemicals, phosphates and 'active washing ingredients'. Several companies make products that clean effectively and leave fewer harmful residues in the water and soil.

www.ecover.com
In 1993, Ecover, the world's largest producer of eco-friendly cleaning products, was awarded the United Nations Environment Programme's Global 500 Award. In 1992, the company built the world's first ecological factory, which is one of the opening images on this site. Use this site to find out what cleaning and personal-care products they offer, and where to buy them in your area.

www.ecoverb2b.co.uk/products.htm
Non-toxic cleaning products for professional cleaners.

http://es.epa.gov/techinfo/facts/safe-fs.html
What's toxic in household cleaners and what you could use instead.

www.greenbrands.co.uk
Earth-friendly cleaning products for the home and office.

www.simplegreen.co.uk
Biodegradable, non-toxic cleaning products for house-holds and commercial cleaners.

CLIMATE CHANGE

SEE ALSO: Action, Architecture, Business, Energy, Environment, Global Warming

Everyone is talking about it, but talking is not enough. We have to start addressing the very serious problems that climate change is bringing to ecosystems the world over.

www.carbonsense.org
The problem couldn't be clearer. Senior business managers should take **the carbon journey**. There's help for those interested in building a **carbon-zero community**, and workshops in **other projects** to help spread the word. This is something we all must get behind. Those in **about us** are inspirational. Denial is not an option.

www.climateark.org
Climate Ark is an Internet search engine accessing information gathered from all over the world that clearly lays out the growing impact of global warming and its effect on global climates.

www.climatecare.org

Climate Care enables you to calculate the amount of carbon emissions that result from your activities, and provides a mechanism by which the damage caused by those emissions can be offset. **Offsets made simple** in **about us** explains why carbon offsets are essential, and how they are achieved. Click on **projects** to see how your offset is changing people's lives, or reforesting the land. The next time you fly, estimate your carbon emissions on the calculator in the sidebar, and then make a contribution to help the climate.

www.climatechallenge.gov.uk

'Tomorrow's climate is today's challenge' is the strapline of this excellent site, dedicated to helping all of us **understand** what climate change is, how it will affect us, and how we can **communicate** the importance of the issue to others. **Get involved** has the tools you will need to spread the word. There are excellent **animations** for children, and a **film** to show your friends. If you have a good idea about how to communicate this essential information to the public to encourage them to start taking steps to counteract the effects of climate change, then you should explore the possibility of funding by clicking on the **climate challenge fund**.

www.climatewire.org

This daily news service delivers articles about climate change from all over the English-speaking world.

www.naturescalendar.org.uk

Help scientists monitor **climate change** by recording your observations of Nature – when the first cuckoo calls, or when the first bluebell dances in a wood near you – and join the **enature blog** to record your own nature diary.

www.theclimategroup.org

An international coalition of governments and companies committed to cutting greenhouse gases, while increasing financial growth. **Reducing emissions** has information on how it's being achieved. **News and events** will keep you up to date, and there are many interesting downloadable pdfs in **information centre**.

www.whatyoucando.co.uk

Use the advice and products on this site and start taking action against the impact of climate change.

COFFEE

SEE ALSO: Fairtrade

The industrial methods of growing coffee involve extensive deforestation to provide land for coffee plantations, which destroys the trees in the wintering grounds of migratory songbirds, and creates a monoculture that has to be supported by chemical pesticides and fertilizers. Shade-grown coffee is cultivated in the traditional way, under a forest canopy that preserves the natural habitat needed for migratory songbirds and other creatures. Fairtrade coffee is coffee produced by farmers who are paid fairly, thus ensuring the economic health and well-being of their families and the wider community. When you buy coffee, support companies that produce and sell shade-grown, organic, Fairtrade brands.

www.alotofcoffee.co.uk

This site, which offers organic, Fairtrade coffee, tea and chocolate as well as chocolate-covered espresso beans, chocolate bars and biscuits, would be a good place to start when ordering for the office coffee-maker.

www.cafedirect.com

Cafédirect markets Fairtrade coffee, tea and cocoa produced in eleven countries by over a quarter of a million growers. **Products** lists what's available and where you can buy it. **Growers** tells the story of how effective this organization has been in restoring the well-being of small producers all over the world, by always paying them more than the world market price. That means the producers get a fair price. **Out of home** has information for businesses, restaurants and hotels that buy coffee in bulk. Click on **Fairtrade** and find out why groups like Cafédirect should be supported.

www.fairtrade.org.uk/products_coffee.htm

The Fairtrade organization started out fighting for the right of coffee-growers to be paid fairly for what they produced. Their report *Spilling the Beans*, which outlines the differences between traditionally traded coffee and coffee that is fairly traded, is essential reading for all coffee drinkers. **Range and availability** lists the many places where you can buy Fairtrade coffee.

http://magazine.audubon.org/features0408/mexico.html

An article about the connection between shade-grown coffee and birds.

www.risc.org.uk/readingroom/coffee.html
While you are enjoying your morning coffee, you might browse through the links on this page. They present a broad coverage of the debate about social responsibility and the global economy, with particular reference to the issue of how your coffee was produced and marketed.

COMMUNITY

SEE ALSO: Action, Compost, Eden Project, Sustainable Living, Volunteering

www.care2.com
To build a community you need to be connected. This compendium of sites offers news, environmental information, shopping, jokes and free cards, plus an active online community offering discussion groups, photo-swapping and companionship. So get connected and make a difference.

www.communityforest.org.uk
England's Community Forests is regenerating local forests all over the country. **Your local forest** will link to the site of the one nearest you. Get involved, and help to make a forest that will bring pleasure to you and your grandchildren's children.

www.est.org.uk/cafe/welcome
Community Action for Energy is for those who want to improve the environment of their local community. Join the **discussion forum**, learn how to run a community

energy project in **resources and information**, and click on **links** for more connections.

www.greendrinks.org

Meet up with fellow environmentalists and plan the world of the future over a drink.

www.greenhousetrust.co.uk

The Greenhouse in Norwich shows what can be achieved with resolve and huge community effort. A dilapidated old building was restored through the help of the Greenhouse Trust and the loving labour of many, and is now a centre of environmental excellence where people can come and learn what is possible. **About the Greenhouse** has the history. **Environmental features** shows what can be done. The **café** serves organic food and Fairtrade teas and coffee, with plenty of books to read, and **environmental information** is what it's all about. Click on **services** if you want to use one of the two meeting rooms for a gathering.

www.simpleliving.net

Another cyberspace community – connect with others and let the hundreds of links on this site help you live a simpler and perhaps happier life.

www.worldchanging.com

This site connects those who are working for a better, healthier, greener future. It highlights the technologies that can enable us to live more sustainably, and is building an internet community of people who will collaborate and share their knowledge of those technologies. As they say, 'Changing the world is a team sport.' Browsing through the hugely diverse subjects covered on this site is to wander around the world discovering all the amazing things going on that can change the way we live. Join the crowd, and add your contribution.

COMPOST

··

SEE ALSO: Eden Project, Educate Yourself, Environment, Farming, Gardens, Reduce-Reuse-Recycle, Sustainable Living, Teachers, Worms

Compost your household food waste and see how your garden grows.

··

www.communitycompost.org
The Community Composting Network supports all those involved in the composting of organic waste, from allotment-holders and individual gardeners to those running not-for-profit community schemes. **About us** explains the benefits of such activity, and how it works. **Info** has guides to both home and community composting.

www.journeytoforever.org/compost.html
This wonderful site has everything you need to know to get started, with information on indoor and outdoor composting and school composting projects, as well as solar box cookers and growing silk worms in a box.

www.recyclenow.com/compost
All the wonders of composting are here in this RecycleNow composting page. There's a **composting guide** to help the

newcomers, and the **latest news and articles** for those who are old hands. **Using your compost** has advice on where to put it when it's matured.

COMPOSTING TOILETS

SEE ALSO: Eden Project, Sustainable Living

Fresh water is rapidly becoming a scarce natural resource. According to Thames Water, one third of household water is used to flush the toilet. Composting toilets use little or no water, have no connection to sewage systems, and produce an end product that is safe, healthy and beneficial to gardens.

www.clivus.com/index.html
Clivus Multrum composting toilets are found all over the world.

compostingtoilet.org/compost_toilets_explained/index.php
Composting toilets explained.

www.natsol.co.uk
English composting-toilet specialists. **Products** and **examples** show their range.

COMPUTERS

SEE ALSO: London, Reduce-Reuse-Recycle

www.computersforcharity.org.uk

Don't throw your redundant computer systems into the landfill. **Donate** them to Computers for Charity, who will pick them up, wipe their memories, refurbish them and sell them to people who need them. Community groups and others **looking** for computer systems might find one here.

www.itforcharities.co.uk/pcs.htm

If you want to get rid of an old computer, link up with an organization on this list and donate it. Don't throw it away.

www.lowtech.org

Art and technology combine in imaginative ways with this Sheffield group, Redundant Technologies Inc. At **Access Space**, they will **recycle** your discarded computers to **create** art and teach web-design skills.

www.2ndchancepc.co.uk

If you need another computer, scroll down to the bottom of the page and click on **refurbished computers**.

CONSCIOUS CONSUMERISM

SEE ALSO: Climate Change, Energy, Fairtrade, Fish, Food, Gifts, Nappies, Peak Oil, Pesticides and Toxins, Plastic and Alternatives, Reduce-Reuse-Recycle, Shopping Bags, Sustainable Living, Waste, Water

Being aware of how our purchases are produced and how much waste we create will help us protect the quality of our water, soil and air, and the future of our grandchildren's children. If we want to maintain our high standard of living, we need to start using energy-efficient products and fuel-efficient cars, reduce industrial and agricultural pollution, and consider the long-term effects of the methods of production of everything we buy. That is what 'conscious consumerism' is all about.

www.ecocentric.co.uk
Sustainably produced beauty for the home and office is the central ethos of EcoCentric. There are coasters made from recycled coffee cups and yoghurt pots, pool balls recycled into salt and pepper shakers, and cushion covers made from recycled seatbelts. Anything is possible in a world where 'waste' becomes a resource. Buy a solar iPod-charger in **eco office**. To find out why conscious consumerism is important, click on **eco info**.

www.eco-furniture.co.uk
Furniture made from locally and sustainably grown ash thinnings (young trees cleared to let more light into the forest), which are moulded into shape by steaming. Thus, waste becomes a raw material, while the production method saves energy. Click on **who is Roy** to find out

more. **Sustainable design** will introduce you to other furniture-makers using renewable resources and waste as their raw material.

www.ethical-company-organisation.org
Order your copy of *The Good Shopping Guide* from this site – an essential tool for the conscious consumer.

www.ethicalconsumer.org
This website is run by the Ethical Consumer Research Association (ECRA), a not-for-profit workers' cooperative that helps consumers to make choices that will sustain the Earth and our fellow human beings. Scroll down to **introduction to ethical consumerism** for the philosophy behind the organization. **Buyers' guides** has an array of reports arranged alphabetically on many products and services, some of which are free and some of which you pay for. **Ethiscore** rates products from nought to twenty, and **corporate critic** is a research database measuring the ethical responsibility of over fifteen thousand companies. Subscribe to the magazine and keep up to date.

www.gooshing.co.uk
The Good Shopping Guide's free ethical shopping guide offers assessments of over 250,000 products. Use this tool to find out how socially and environmentally responsible the products you want to buy are, while you compare prices. In **food and drink** there are lists of local and organic suppliers. **Home energy** will help you find a supplier of 'green' electricity. **Ratings** explains how the system works. If you are buying a property, click on **money** to find out about green mortgages and ethical investing.

www.nigelsecostore.com

More eco-friendly products for the home and office. **Laundry and cleaning** offers the amazing E-cloths – microfibre, non-toxic cleaning cloths that just need water to be effective. I use them all the time. **Eco office** has water-powered clocks and calculators and PC monitors, mice and keypads made from bamboo. A broadband videophone can help you cut down on travel, one of the biggest causes of greenhouse gas pollution.

www.pbs.org/kcts/affluenza

Affluenza is a one-hour film that explores the high costs of consumerism to our society and the environment around the world. It shows men and women across America, where consumerism is rampant, who have decided to spend more time with friends and family and not allow the drive to acquire more things dominate their lives. This site analyses the problems of over-consumption, with good suggestions for treatment. Learn about the film, order it, download discussion guidelines, and plan an evening sharing it with your friends.

www.worldwatch.org/features/consumption

Worldwatch Institute's in-depth examination of the what, why and how of consumption. There's a video to watch, and **Good stuff? A behind-the-scenes guide to the things to buy.**

CONSERVATION

....

SEE ALSO: Birds, Biodiversity, Coral Reefs, Endangered Species, Environment, Frogs, Fungi, National Parks, Oceans, Pollinators, Trees, Tourism, Volunteering

It is becoming increasingly clear that if we want our children to live in a world as productive and diverse as the one we were born into, the conservation of that world is of vital importance. Availability of water, renewable energy, the protection of waterways and wetlands, marine-resource protection, land clearing, climate change, aquaculture, forest and wilderness management, oceans and coasts, continuing biodiversity, pollution and waste are all issues that are central to conservation, because the Earth's natural systems are the producers of the natural capital upon which our economic survival depends.

....

www.bats.org.uk

Though bats are sometimes feared and vilified, they benefit humans by killing insects and pollinating plants. The UK's seventeen species are all protected, and the Bat Conservation Trust's mission is to help humans get along with bats, thus ensuring their survival. If you have them in your house, there is information in **ask us your bat questions** as to how to deal with them without hurting them. If you want bats in your garden to control night-flying insects, **practical bat conservation** will tell you how to attract them. **Bat kids** has lots of great bat facts, and if you want to **help count bats**, there's a field survey tutorial to get you started.

www.bbc.co.uk/nature/animals/conservation

This BBC site has beautiful images, and wide-ranging information about the status of animal life on Earth. **Planet Earth** has pictures to download for screensavers and desktops. Click on any animal featured for a comprehensive list of links to help you understand how each species is doing in the struggle for survival. Make your own films and improve your editing skills by using the information and footage freely available on **the open earth archive**.

www.butterfly-conservation.org

Butterfly Conservation is working to protect and restore our indigenous moths and butterflies, whose numbers are in serious decline due to the destruction of their habitat through agriculture, urban development and poor land care. **Introduction** links you to all aspects of the organization's **conservation** activities, the **butterflies** and **moths** they are conserving, and **how you can help**.

www.earthwatch.org/europe

Since 1971, Earthwatch has been offering volunteers the chance to participate in scientific expeditions worldwide that focus on conservation. Three principles underlie their mission: the gathering of independent scientific data; the importance of education as a tool for sustainable living; and the importance of our responsibility to future generations of all global species. **Expedition search** offers an endless list of possibilities – from lost kingdoms to whales, caterpillars to coral reefs, butterflies to lions, Roman forts to basking sharks – all waiting to be explored.

www.floralocale.org

Over the last century, industrial agriculture and urban development practices have devastated huge areas of wetlands, ancient forests and wildflower meadows. Flora Locale wants to restore destroyed native plant communities. **Issues** summarizes the problem, and **action plan** presents solutions. **Projects** shows where the wildflowers are already being re-established. Those interested in learning more about wildflower management will find extensive resources in the **knowledge zone** and there are many links to other organizations focusing on restorative horticulture. Anyone interested in growing a wildflower garden should read the information in **suppliers** and then order their seeds from the list provided.

www.landlife.org.uk

Landlife is bringing the country to the town by developing wildflower areas in urban and urban-fringe communities. They sell **seeds and plants** grown in their wildflower nursery, and you can see what they have been planting in **projects**. If you are in the vicinity of Liverpool between March and September, visit their **National Wildlife Centre** and decide what you'd like to see flourishing in your garden.

www.rbgkew.org.uk/conservation/index.html

This is the conservation page of the Royal Botanical Gardens at Kew, who are developing conservation strategies to help preserve the world's plant diversity. The Millennium Seedbank at Wakehurst Place in West Sussex is at the heart of this enterprise. Click on **seed conservation** to find out more.

www.treesforlife.org.uk
The once great Caledonian forest in Scotland is a shadow of its former self, and this group is determined to ensure its survival. In 2005, volunteers planted the 500,000th tree, and anyone interested in helping plant the next 500,000 should click on **volunteer work weeks**.

www.wwf.org.uk
The World Wildlife Fund has taken the lead in many conservation efforts. Click on **one planet living** in the list of **campaigns** to learn how to live in a way that does not consume more resources than this one planet of ours can offer.

CONSUMER WEB WATCH

www.consumerwebwatch.com
The Consumer Web Watch is a service provided by the Consumers' Union in the United States to help you monitor the credibility of information published on the Internet.

CORAL REEFS

SEE ALSO: Action, Oceans, Tourism

Coral reefs are among the world's most endangered yet most productive ecosystems. They have worldwide economic significance. However, coral reefs everywhere are being destroyed by multiple forces: global warming, which causes bleaching; pollution from agricultural run-off and human waste; sedimentation from coastal development, dredging, deforestation and bad agricultural practices; and over-harvesting, largely because of illegal fishing techniques that use dynamite and cyanide. What you can do is to lobby governments to support treaties and international agreements that protect this irreplaceable treasure; avoid buying wild-caught, tropical, salt-water aquarium fish, and support companies that only sell artificial coral for aquariums. If you're a diver or snorkeller, learn techniques that don't harm coral reefs.

---

www.gbrmpa.gov.au
The Great Barrier Reef is the largest protected marine area and World Heritage Site in the world. This website is full of information about this unique place.

www.mesa.edu.au/sites/coral_reefs.asp
The **Coral links** page from the Marine Education Society of Australasia has links to reefs all over the world, and is a good resource for teachers. Pictures for projects can be downloaded on **reef snapshots**.

www.reefbase.org
This global portal for information on coral reefs has extensive data on the location, status, management and threats faced by coral reefs worldwide.

D

DEATH

www.ac026.dial.pipex.com/naturaldeath
The Natural Death Centre is a charity that can help you arrange an inexpensive, environmentally friendly funeral.

www.eco-coffin.co.uk
Elegant eco-friendly coffins made from a mixture of wood pulp certified by the Forest Stewardship Council (FCS) and recycled paper, with woven cotton handles.

www.nigelsecostore.com/acatalog/eco-after-life.html
Instead of choosing a conventional coffin, why not consider a sustainable ecopod or an acorn urn made from 100 per cent recycled non-toxic materials as a final resting place for your loved one?

www.uk-funerals.co.uk/green-funerals.html
This site offers a beautiful wicker-basket coffin, plus a list of woodland burial grounds scattered throughout the UK.

DESIGN

··

SEE ALSO: Architecture, Eden Project, Natural Laws, Sustainable Living

··

www.green.net.au/srd

Everything we use has a lasting impact on the Earth. Designers need to consider their materials, the manufacturing process they put those materials through, the life of their creation, and what happens at the end of that life. The Society for Responsible Design from Australia addresses these questions and offers a list of suggestions to help promote sustainably responsible design, in the areas of graphics, interior design and apparel.

www.solarlab.org

The future in the present. Solar Lab designed the solar-powered boat that is now glittering its silent, pollution-free way across the Serpentine in Hyde Park. In **projects** there are beautiful pictures of other solar-powered boats, floating solar buildings, and buildings that turn, like sunflowers, to follow the sun.

www.xco2.com

This London-based environmental engineering consultancy believes that low CO_2 emissions and elegance of design go hand in hand. They are a carbon-neutral business. **Projects** include the restoration of old buildings to include wind and solar energy; a planned rain-shelter over a go-karting track in Mile End Park that doubles as one the UK's largest solar-power stations; a demountable and zero-carbon exhibition space; low-energy design strategies for urban schools; development of reliable, 100 per cent renewable energy from sustainable resources for new urban developments; low-energy housing designs; and their award-winning photovoltaic roof tiles. **Quiet revolution** introduces you to their vertical-axis wind turbine. Designed for urban use, it utilizes winds from all directions with almost no noise or vibration.

DRY-CLEANING

The normal dry-cleaning process uses a man-made substance commonly known as perchlorethylene (PERC), which is a possible human carcinogen. Because of concerns for the health of dry-cleaning operators and their customers, there are healthier alternatives to PERC beginning to come on to the market.

www.earth911.org/usa/master.asp?s=lib&a=shopsmart/tech.html
Wet-cleaning, a healthy alternative to dry-cleaning, is now available in Canada, the USA and Europe. This article explains the process and offers a list of wet-cleaners in the States. Electrolux and Firbimatic have introduced wet-cleaning machines to the UK, so perhaps an environmentally minded entrepreneur might consider opening a chain of wet-cleaning stores in the UK.

www.greenearth.co.uk
GreenEarth cleaning uses a solution based on silica to dry-clean your clothes. Click on **nearest branch** to find your nearest green dry-cleaner.

www.lotusorganics.com/articles/greendrycleaning.aspx
Dry-cleaning in a nutshell.

E

EDEN PROJECT

www.edenproject.com

After a recent trip to the Eden Project, a Vermont friend said to me, 'The artfulness and creativity used to communicate their message is unparalleled. It is unlike any other place on Earth.' Since the Eden Visitor Centre first welcomed the public in 2001, over eight million people of all ages have encountered this visionary world, where art, science, technology, performance, education and, above all, plants flourish. **Horticulture** shows the soaring **humid tropics biome**, the **warm temperate biome** and the **outside biome**, all encompassing the message at the heart of the project – that without plants we die.

Use this site to book a visit to this living laboratory that encourages us to treasure the soil, work as a team and have fun while we learn how we fit into Earth's living systems. The Eden Project educates our future leaders, and wraps up a gloriously inspirational day with a concert in what the *Independent* declared was the best rock venue in the UK.

EDUCATE YOURSELF

If we want our children to inherit a healthy planet, we need to realize that our individual actions matter, and start making educated and responsible decisions. However, in order to make those decisions, we need reliable information.

www.earth-policy.org

Knowing that our needs have outstripped the Earth's capacity to supply them, Lester Brown, one of our most influential thinkers, is actively campaigning for us to replace our present economic system, based on fossil fuel, with one based on renewable energy and other sustainable technologies. The electronic news service is excellent, and **Plan B 2.0** is inspirational.

www.earthtrends.wri.org

Use the World Resources Institute's portal to access its extensive database for information on the environmental, social and economic trends that are shaping our world.

www.environmentaldefense.org

Environmental Defense does just that. Since 1967 it has worked with its team of scientists, lawyers and economists to ensure clean air, healthy water, a rich biosphere and a better future for life on Earth. They have shared such successes as phasing out the lead in petrol and establishing safe-drinking-water standards. **Programs** has solid scientific information about the most urgent issues. Check out **partnerships** and see what they are doing with companies such as FedEx and McDonald's.

www.nationalgeographic.com/earthpulse

Immerse yourself in this site's rich offerings of pictures, stories and the sounds of Planet Earth. Visit the interactive reef, kelp, suburban, rainforest and river habitats by clicking on **virtual worlds**. Use the themes in **conservation** to learn more about our effect on Planet Earth.

www.peopleandplanet.net

This excellent site has stories and articles from all over the world about the continual pressure that humans' needs are placing upon the natural world. The photos in **picture gallery** – covering such topics as hydrogen-fuel-cell buses, farmers in East Mali growing crops in bare rocks, great white sharks, child labour and biogas projects in India – all have links to further information. In **poems** there are links to poetry inspired by environmental issues, written by children.

www.rmi.org

The Rocky Mountain Institute is one of the world's leading non-profit environmental organizations. It works with governments, communities, businesses and individuals to help them rebuild their economies using the principles of energy efficiency and natural capitalism. **Areas of impact** is a good place to start. **Home resource efficiency** in **buildings and land** has a thorough analysis of the steps needed to create an energy-efficient home.

www.royalsoc.ac.uk
The Royal Society is the UK's independent and world-renowned academy of science. In **science issues** you will find information about climate change, energy, the environment, GM crops and many other issues.

uk.oneworld.net
The *Guardian* says that 'OneWorld is a constantly evolving window on some of the most serious issues facing the world today.' There are 'two million pages of text, images, audio and video content produced by 1,600 partners, 1,000 broadcasters and 6,000 video-makers' contained in this site, creating a global network of activists working for justice, health, the environment and other social issues that are central to our lives.

www.worldwatch.org
Their annual State of the World Report is a classic.

ENDANGERED SPECIES

SEE ALSO: Biodiversity, Conservation, Pollinators

Every seven and a half minutes Earth loses another species. And with that loss, another link in the invisible chain of life, which humans are part of and depend upon for survival, vanishes. For ever. Not all these species are big animals, although some, like our nearest relatives the primates, are endangered. We are losing many organisms vital to the health of soil, on which all plant life depends, in addition to animals and plants that have yet to be discovered. Loss of species is a good measure of human impact on the Earth's biodiversity.

www.arkive.org
The Noah's Ark of the Internet. Wildscreen's audio-visual record of life on Earth has an infinite number of beautiful images. Photographic and audio records of more than fifteen thousand endangered species from all over the world are being collected in this archive for us all to see and hear.

www.cites.org/gallery/species/index.html
The Convention on International Trade in Endangered Species of Wild Flora and Fauna (CITES) is one of the most effective laws we have for protecting endangered species, many of which can be seen in this photo gallery.

www.iucnredlist.org
The World Conservation Union's IUCN Red Data Book and Red List are the ultimate authority on what species now need protection from humans.

www.rhinos-irf.org
Less than 17,500 rhinos are alive in the wild today. Some species are down to just a handful of survivors. The International Rhino Foundation works to protect those that are left.

www.well.com/user/davidu/extinction.html
Telling it like it is. This site, a comprehensive source of information on the mass extermination of species, is an altogether sobering experience.

ENERGY

SEE ALSO: Architecture, Building Green, Business, Climate Change, Community, Conscious Consumerism, Design, Farming, Films, Global Warming, Home, Hydrogen Fuel Cells, Lighting, Nuclear, Sustainable Living

'No other issue intersects with a wider variety of environmental problems than what kind of energy we employ to empower society, where we get it, and how efficiently we use it.' Earth Day Guide to Planet Repair.

More than one quarter of the total carbon-dioxide emissions in the UK come from household use, and demand keeps growing. The simplest way to save energy is to start using it efficiently, and to turn off anything that does not need to be switched on. Electricity from renewable resources is now readily available, and as customers we must request it. If enough of us do so, the collective impact on the growth of cheap, renewable energy will be enormous. Buy products with the Energy Saving Recommended label, or which carry a European Energy Rating label – the highest is A (or in the case of fridges and freezers, A+, A++) and the lowest is G – a high rating guarantees that the product will save energy, cost less to run and help the environment.

www.ecologicalhosting.com

The data centre that operates this website server is run on solar power. If your web-hosting service is due for renewal, perhaps you should consider this one that uses renewable energy to send the messages out.

www.ecotricity.co.uk
Ecotricity offers you the 'single biggest step you could take to reduce your impact in the environment'. This energy company invests in the creation of new sources of renewable energy, and are building **wind parks** in many parts of the UK. Companies interested in building wind turbines in conjunction with Ecotricity should click on **merchant wind power** and see who else has done it.

www.electrisave.co.uk
This smart little tool not only shows you exactly how much electricity each device in your house is using at any one time, but also how much it is costing you and the amount of greenhouse gas being generated. Install one in your home or business, and learn how you can save electricity, money and the Earth, all at the same time.

www.est.org.uk
The Energy Saving Trust is tackling climate change head on. You may know it through its energy-saving recommended mark, used on over 1,800 products for the home and businesses. The Trust, which promotes the use of energy-efficient techniques in homes, businesses and transport, is the UK's representative in the European Energy Network, working to develop imaginative solutions for a more sustainable Europe. Click on **about EST** and then **what we do** to discover the range of programmes offered, and to read about their policy initiatives that will help achieve an energy-efficient, carbon-neutral way of life. There are tips to help you **save 20 per cent** of your everyday energy use. **Rise of the machines** is an in-depth analysis of the impact that domestic appliances are having and will have on climate change. Local authorities, housing providers,

home-owners, builders, schools and businesses will find a wealth of ideas, advice and support, as well as information about grants and funding, on this excellent site.

www.good-energy.co.uk

Good Energy supplies renewable electricity generated by wind, solar and small-scale hydro generators to customers all over Britain. Downloadable price lists and online quotes are available. **Home generation** informs businesses and home-owners how they can be paid for every unit of electricity they generate from renewable microgeneration systems. **Spread the word** offers rewards for those who encourage their friends to sign up and save an annual average of two tonnes of carbon-dioxide emissions by using electricity from renewable sources. **Good advice** has excellent energy-saving tips. **What you can do** in **climate change** clearly states how the little we can all do to lower carbon-dioxide emissions really does make a difference.

www.greenelectricity.org

One of the easiest steps on the path to sustainable living is to switch to green electricity. This site puts you in touch with who's offering it, what it costs, and how to sign up.

www.grownupgreen.org.uk/library/?id=282

GrownupGreen and Solar Century talk about the benefits of solar power. Read this, and you'll want a solar roof.

www.navitron.org.uk

Navitron offers a wide range of affordable alternative-energy technology. Ask your questions and share your knowledge in the **forum**, and there are some interesting sites in **links**.

www.niesmart.co.uk/microtariff.htm

The Northern Ireland Electricity Smart programme is designed to help householders and businesses generate electricity from renewable sources. **Micro renewable generation** has details of a reward scheme for the unused energy produced and exported from the point of generation. There are **renewable grants for homes** available. **News** has stories of schools, homes, businesses and even a church plugging into the sun and wind for their energy.

www.renewabledevices.com

Renewable Devices are the designers and manufacturers of the award-winning Swift Wind Turbine that can be mounted on the roof of your house like a satellite dish. It is 'quiet and vibration-free', and can provide 'approximately one third of the electricity requirements of the average two-bedroom house'.

www.rspbenergy.co.uk

The Royal Society for the Protection of Birds offers green energy, e-billing, advice on energy efficiency and much more. Do it for the birds.

www.solarcentury.com

Solar Century envisions solar panels on the roof of every building, supplying clean energy for a sustainable future – a vision they believe can be fulfilled within this generation. **Who we are** explains that vision, and **walking our talk** demonstrates how they are doing it. **Projects** shows what is possible, and **news** will keep you up to date. **Homeowners** has information on possible grants to help you install a solar system on your roof.

www.thewind.info/body.html
If you have concerns about the effects of wind turbines on bird mortality, click on **briefings** and read the report.

ENVIRONMENT
....

SEE ALSO: every other entry in this book

The environment is not something separate from ourselves, it is us. It is the world in which we live. We are the environment. No issue is more important, for without a healthy environment, life will not be worth living.

....

www.3acorns.co.uk
If you have decided to live sustainably but are not sure where to start, then Donnachadh McCarthy might be just the person you need. He has travelled that path and now offers his extensive knowledge to help others start the same journey. Begin by buying a copy of the excellent book *Saving the Planet without Costing the Earth* to use as a travel guide.

www.defra.gov.uk
The work of the Department of Environment, Food and Rural Affairs (DEFRA) is central to the improvement of the environmental standards of the air we breathe, the water we drink and swim in, our food and the health of those who produce it, the land on which we live, and the biodiversity of all the other species sharing that land with us. This site has many resources for the

individual, and also those interested in the government policies connected with these areas.

www.environment-agency.gov.uk

The Environment Agency is working to protect and improve all aspects of the environmental health of England and Wales, and its site is full of links to help you be part of that process. **About us** sets out the agency's **vision** for a cleaner, more sustainable world. There are links to all current environmental issues. You can get a fishing licence, find out where to use it, and, more importantly, learn how to **save fish** in drought. Water is vital to living systems, and **water resources** has many links to assist homes, businesses, industry and the public sector to conserve and use sustainably the water we have. Click on **your environment** and find out **what's in your backyard**.

www.greenchoices.org

Green choices are choices that take the environment into consideration as well as our needs and wants. Use this site to find green choices for the home, for holidays and for work.

www.wen.org.uk

The Women's Environmental Network believes in educating, empowering, researching and taking action on behalf of a greener, healthier world for all. **Beauty within, beauty without** connects you to their campaign on ingredients in cosmetics. Their **real nappies project**, which raises awareness of the benefits of cloth nappies and the polluting effects of disposables, is getting stronger every year. There are downloadable pdfs to encourage the proper handling of **waste**. The many environmental issues connected with tampons and disposable liners are addressed in **sanpro**. Their campaigns for healthy **food** support the transformation of wasteground into healthy community gardens, where local women can grow their own food; working with schools to teach children how to garden; the development of local farmers' markets, as well as the wider issues of GM foods and food miles – the distance food travels to get on to your plate. The **resources** links in all of these categories are excellent.

PEOPLE WHO DID

IT WAS AN encounter with the reclusive Yanomami Indians who live deep in the Amazon rainforest of Venezuela that began **Donnachadh McCarthy**'s transformation from a Royal Opera House dancer with no awareness of green issues into an environmental activist and politician. During the month he spent with these forest-dwellers he observed two things: that the Yanomami had lived in their area for over twenty thousand years without causing any environmental impact, and that their ancient, stable and beautiful way of life was now being threatened by the demands on their habitat being made by our aggressive, Western, consumerist way of life.

Donnachadh came back home determined to start making more conscious choices about the way he lived. He started recycling, he made sure that there was always something organic in his basket whenever he went to the supermarket, and he became active in a campaign to save a local park from the developers. It was through that campaign that his environmental activism began to flourish, and even though he had no training in how to approach the complicated world of political decision-making, he just waded in and started making phone calls, attending meetings, and speaking up in his community. His environmental education took off as well, as he learned more and more from his new colleagues about how our mindless consumption continues to strain Earth's resources beyond its capacity to support us. As he became increasingly involved, he stopped dancing, bought a computer, joined the Liberal Democrats, and in 1994 was elected to Southwark Council.

By now his political and environmental skills were well honed and he started advocating the building of new homes that were energy and water efficient, with rain-catching barrels and composting units in the garden. But he didn't stop there. Within four years he was elected to the National Executive of the Liberal Democrats and became an integral part of the team developing progressive environmental policies on matters such as the labelling of GM foods and their removal from animal food, and pesticide-reduction strategies. He rose to be Deputy Chair, but then left to concentrate on his growing environmental mission.

Donnachadh has written an excellent book, *Saving the Planet without Costing the Earth*, which should be on every bedside table. He writes articles and is an environmental commentator for TV and radio, but what is best is that he practises what he preaches. His Peckham house has solar heating and photovoltaic cells, 85 per cent of his household water comes from collected rainwater, all his light bulbs are energy saving, he sells electricity back to the grid from his photovoltaic cells and roof wind turbine, plants a tree each time he travels, and has reduced his waste to one small bag a month.

When Donnachadh McCarthy began his journey to a sustainable lifestyle, he applied what he knew as a dancer—the daily repetition of the basic steps will take you to the highest leap. If we all follow his example and start to take small steps daily to live with less impact on our Earth, then we too will share his deep pleasure in knowing that our lives are better, richer and more fulfilled, and that our grandchildren will not inherit a depleted, degraded and uninhabitable home.

F

FAIRTRADE

See also: Coffee

Fairtrade is the means of guaranteeing that artisans and farmers are paid fairly for what they make and grow. By buying direct from these small-scale producers, rather than through international commodity markets, Fairtrade Associations are able to promote better health, childcare, education, environmental stewardship and development among these communities. Next time you go shopping, look for the Fairtrade label, and support small-scale producers.

www.fairtrade.org.uk

The UK Fairtrade Foundation is part of an international group of organizations promoting fair trade. Look in **products** for what's available, and where the products can be bought. There are even recipes.

www.traidcraft.co.uk

This Christian charity uses a combination of activism and marketing to champion Fairtrade. Anyone wanting to sell Fairtrade products will find help in **become a Fair Trader**. You can go shopping on **products** or, if you'd like a walk, check **retailers near you**. If you're looking for a speaker for your next event, **speaker scheme** offers some suggestions. Traidcraft won the 2006 Queen's Award for Industry for Sustainable Development.

FARMING

SEE ALSO: **Compost, Food, Gardens, Health, Meat, Peak Oil, Pesticides and Toxins, Plastic and Alternatives, Pollinators, Trees, Volunteering, Waste, Water**

www.commondreams.org/views02/0729-01.htm
An article from the *Los Angeles Times* about the effect of industrialized farming on productive land, which has universal relevance.

www.pmac.net/AM/no_blackouts.html
An American dairy farmer describes in *American Farm Bureau News* the benefits of converting methane extracted from manure to electricity. Our electricity at home in Vermont comes from cows.

www.rspb.org.uk/countryside/farming/index.asp
Wildlife-habitat and species-management advice for farmers from the Royal Society for the Protection of Birds.

www.soilassociation.org/foodandfarming
This Soil Association site is for anyone wanting to be an organic farmer or horticulturalist. They offer **training events**, answer questions with **technical information**, offer resources for all branches of agriculture, **certification** and **marketing information**, and **members**

get even more. **Local food** has advice for those interested in selling their produce through community-supported agriculture (CSA).

FILMS

See also: X Chromosome

www.endofsuburbia.com
Suburbs without cars won't be much fun, but as this film tells us in no uncertain terms, that is what we face when the petrol runs out.

www.freerangegraphics.com
Free Range Graphics makes witty, animated films addressing environmental issues. When you see the chicken, click on **gallery**, then **flash movies**. I particularly enjoy *The Meatrix*, *Save Chilean Sea Bass* and *The Cycle of Violence*.

www.green.tv
Green TV has partnered with UNEP and others to bring a wide variety of films dealing with environmental issues to your computer via broadband. The director Ade Thomas calls it 'green google for green films'. If you'd like to add your film to the list, click on **info**.

FISH

··

SEE ALSO: Action, Films, Oceans, Schools

Seventy-five per cent of the world's fisheries are either exploited to their maximum capacity or over-exploited. In the last fifty years, industrial fishing practices have wiped out 90 per cent of tuna, halibut, swordfish and grouper. Some fisheries could disappear before today's five-year-olds have learned to drive. Aquaculture is not the whole answer, since fish-farming practices generally produce polluted waters, and sometimes intensive farming requires the use of antibiotics to keep fish healthy, which then lessens the efficacy of those antibiotics for humans. Escapees from these farms threaten the gene pool of wild populations of the same species. Farmed fish such as shrimp, salmon and tuna require a diet of smaller, wild-caught fish, which further diminishes stocks of those feed species. Also, it is now becoming clear that low-level pollutants in the fish stocks from which the meal that feeds farmed finfish is produced is increasing pollutant levels in that farmed product. Sustainable fishing is the responsibility of consumers as well as governments and industry. We must insist that this nutritious and vital food source is not lost to future generations through the pursuit of short-term economic gain.

··

www.davidsuzuki.org/Oceans/Aquaculture
Renowned Canadian environmentalist David Suzuki's views on aquaculture.

www.ecotrust.org/publications/farmed_salmon_steak.html
An analysis of the ingredients in that deliciously pink farmed salmon steak.

http://eng.msc.org

The Marine Stewardship Council promotes environmentally healthy seafood choices through its MSC label – the only international standard that assures consumers that the fish they are buying has been produced sustainably. Click on **where to buy**, then **United Kingdom** for stores that sell MSC products. **Fisheries** has a link to a list of **certified fisheries** and those **undergoing assessment**, and **fishfacts** explains why certification is necessary. **About MSC** has a link to **fish and kids**, an awareness-raising project for children, schools and the food-service industry.

www.ewg.org/reports/brainfood/sidebar.html

The Environmental Working Group recommends what fish pregnant women should avoid eating because of mercury contamination, and suggests healthier choices. Mercury is toxic to the developing foetal brain, and exposure in the womb can cause delays in mental development and lifelong learning difficulties.

www.fishonline.org

Use the Marine Conservation's resource to help you identify sustainable harvested seafood. For a quick guide to **what to eat** and **what to avoid**, click on **lists**. For more detail, use the **advanced** search. If you need a **glossary**, you'll find one in **information**.

www.foe-scotland.org.uk/nation/fish.html

A report published by Friends of the Earth on 8 January 2004 that highlights a study in *Science* magazine about the high level of PCBs and other pollutants in farmed salmon from Scotland. In some cases the levels of toxicity could outweigh the health benefits provided by eating the fish.

www.gotmercury.org
Whenever I am going to buy fish, I use this guide to determine the probable mercury level in that species. It's easy to use, and although it's a US site, it covers the majority of global fish.

FOOD

SEE ALSO: Compost, Eden Project, Educate Yourself, Farming, Fish, Gardens, Health, London, Meat, Pesticides and Toxins, Plastic and Alternatives, Reduce-Reuse-Recycle, Schools, Sustainable Living, Worms

Eating wholesome food is one of the most effective ways to stay healthy, but one we often forget. It makes sense to avoid foods treated with pesticides, hormones, antibiotics and chemical fertilizers. The question of genetically engineered food is also of concern to people all over the world. The following sites can help you choose which foods are best for you. An easy first step to better health is to buy locally grown, fresh produce.

www.bigbarn.co.uk
Find your suppliers of local food here, and lots of good things to make with it in **recipes**.

www.chronogram.com/issue/2004/11/wholeliving
Before you reach for that diet drink, read this article about artificial sweeteners.

www.commondreams.org/views03/0123-09.htm
Fast-food fascism is an interesting reflection on what

the fast-food movement is doing to our lives and our individualism.

www.foodnews.org

Pesticides are not meant for human consumption. Click on **produce** and download *The Shopper's Guide to Pesticides* – a handy wallet card to help you choose produce that will lower your exposure to pesticides, especially if you are buying food grown in the USA.

www.greenol.co.uk

An online supermarket for organic food products.

www.greenpeace.org.uk/Products/GM/downloads.cfm

If you want to know whether the food you buy contains GM products, **The Shoppers Guide to GM** can help. Download it here and use it when you're shopping.

www.omsco.co.uk

The Organic Milk Suppliers Cooperative lists all the reasons why you and your children should drink organic milk. If you need a break, **stay on a farm** offers some good choices.

www.organicdelivery.co.uk

Certified-organic food and wines delivered to your door by a van powered by used vegetable oil. The Organic Delivery Company of London offers a fresh alternative to the supermarket, and deliciously fresh vegetables. The comments from satisfied customers keep mentioning freshly baked bread. New customers can **register** before ordering from **the shopping aisles**, but check out the bargains in **special offers** first. There's free delivery for orders over £13.95. And when your friends come round for dinner, show them **8 top reasons to go organic.**

www.organicfood.co.uk

Click on **store wars** for an amusing spoof of *Star Wars*, highlighting the benefits of organic food. **Sense** has some interesting articles, and **where to shop** has links to box schemes and shops selling organic produce throughout the UK.

www.safefood.org.nz

Safe Food Campaign is an independent information service to help consumers make informed choices to ensure that their food is healthy. Click on **additives** for an extensive list of what you might not want to eat.

www.seedsofhealth.co.uk

Healthy foods that are locally produced are the focus of this site. Find your nearest farmers' market in **resources**.

www.slowfood.com

The opposite of fast food. This site celebrates the pleasure of enjoying a wealth of tastes in a leisurely fashion. The Slow Food Movement, which started in Italy in 1988, has been putting the dining table back into the centre of our lives, and is now active in over one hundred countries. To find out more about local slow-food groups and events, click on **about us**, then **where we are**, select the **UK** and start enjoying slow food close to home.

www.soilassociation.org.uk

Everything you want to know about the benefits of eating organic food (which is, after all, the way our grandparents ate before the forties) is here in this huge and informative site. The Soil Association has been successfully campaigning for the establishment of organic agriculture for over twenty years. Any product carrying their certification guarantees the consumer that it has been 'produced and processed to strict and rigorous environmental and animal-welfare standards'. **Consumer guide** tells you about those standards, and while you are there, click on **ten reasons to eat organic**. The annual **organic fortnight**, when communities all over the country celebrate the pleasures of organic food, is a great introduction to the organic way of life, and you could spend a rainy afternoon following the many paths offered by the links on the opening page, and end the day refreshed. **Visit an organic farm** and learn why and how observing natural laws is the best way to grow healthy food. Nature trails, farm shops, school visits and overnight stays are also available.

www.sustainweb.org

Sustain, 'the alliance for better food and farming', has many projects advocating the spread of healthy, locally grown and organic foods into the mainstream, through education and changes in public policy. The **grab 5! project** helps schools help their pupils develop a taste for healthier foods. **London food link** encourages restaurateurs to source locally grown food from within the confines of the Tube network. Concern about the availability of these foods for people on low incomes has led to the **food poverty project**, and the importance of healthy hospital food has given rise to the **hospital food project**. There are many policy reports and **publications**, and the **latest news** in the continuing debate on this critical issue.

www.theecologist.org/ archive_detail.asp?content_id=566

Fifteen reasons why you should buy locally produced food.

FOOD FOR BABIES

··

Because babies are small, they eat more per pound of body weight than their parents. Therefore they absorb a greater amount of the chemical residue in non-organically grown foods, which could affect their health later in life. Organic baby food is now readily available, and to give your precious child the best start in life, explore the following sites which offer delicious alternatives to the sugar-and-salt-filled, additive-laden mainstream offerings. The majority are run by parents who wanted organic, additive-free food for their children, and who now have small businesses offering the same to other parents. As well as organic baby food, they offer helpful advice, information and other resources.

··

www.bathorganicbabyfood.co.uk
Truly scrumptious organic baby food made and then fresh-frozen for your baby or toddler. **Stockists** tells you where to buy.

www.daisyfoods.com
Click on **feed me**, get the cookbook, and make your own baby and toddler food.

www.easyfreezy.co.uk
Welsh lamb with apricots is just one of the tasty selections on offer here.

www.hipp.co.uk
Where to buy lists availability in local stores and **abroad**.

www.miniscoff.co.uk

Delicious home-cooked favourites for children from twelve months to twelve years, and their mums and dads too.

www.mums4.com

The *Independent* and the *Daily Mirror* consider Mums4 organic **yogurt** one of the ten best organic baby foods. The **links** section is also one of the best.

www.ulula.co.uk

Biodynamic baby food.

FROGS

SEE ALSO: Gardens

www.froglife.org

If you have seen a frog in your garden, download the **frogwatch** form and send the information to Froglife, who are conducting an ongoing survey about the urban habitats of these amphibians. Frogs are an indicator species, which means that changes in their numbers could indicate a **deterioration** in their habitat, which in turn could be bad news for us. On the other hand, if their numbers are growing, then it's good news all round. There's also a survey for **snakes in the grass**, and **toads on the roads** may need you as a volunteer.

FUNGI

....

*Fungi are fundamental participants in the restoration,
replenishment and healing of ecosystems. Without yeast,
which is a fungus, we wouldn't have bread or beer. Many
antibiotics come from fungi. Yet most of us know very little
about these widespread and important organisms.*

....

www.abfg.org

The depletion of habitat and industrial agriculture are
threatening the survival of many fungi species. The
Association of British Fungus Groups is made up of
amateur enthusiasts who want to help with the
conservation of fungi. If you have seen any of the species
listed in **fungi watch**, let them know. Check out the **latest
list of rare and endangered fungi species**. There's
information about **mushroom hunting**, an **identification
service**, and their magazine, *The Forager*. If **how to find an
ABFG group** doesn't come up with a local group, then
start your own.

www.bms.ac.uk/Code.html

A code of conduct for the harvesting of wild mushrooms.

www.fungi.com/mycotech/mycova.html

Fungi are essential to the health of our soil. This page
explains the benefits of using them to break down organic
matter, and has an interesting story of how oyster
mushrooms grown on soil heavily polluted with oil
restored the health of the soil, and produced an abundant
crop. And what happened next is even more surprising.

G

GARDENS

See also: Birds, Compost, Conservation, Frogs, Health, Pesticides and Toxins, Plastic and Alternatives, Pollinators, Reduce-Reuse-Recycle, Schools, Sustainable Living, Trees, Water, Worms

You can begin to heal the earth in your own back garden by growing your own fruit, flowers and vegetables and providing a home for pollinators, the insects without which we would have no fruit, flowers or vegetables.

www.allotments-uk.com

Growing your own flowers and vegetables is one of the pleasures of life. If you don't have a garden, then use this site to find an allotment, get a spade and start digging. There's tons of **advice**, and a **forum** for your questions and comments.

www.crocus.co.uk

Crocus offers a choice of over three thousand plants, and a follow-up service with reminders and tips to help them flourish. **Introducing crocus** explains the site. Look in **the garden shed** for information on everything ranging from water butts to their free flower-delivery service. Sign up for Alan Titchmarsh's regular email garden tips. Crocus has collaborated with Greenpeace to guarantee that the hardwood furniture they sell is made from sustainably produced timber that has been checked and approved by the Tropical Forest Trust.

www.ecoseeds.co.uk

Ecoseeds, based in Northern Ireland, sells wildflower seeds, and offers its **consultancy and service** to help you restore a profusion of wildlife to your barren site.

www.enviromower.co.uk

A battery-operated, quiet lawnmower. No more tangled electric cords, smelly petrol fumes, or struggles with a pull-cord to start the motor. Even Kensington Palace has one. We have just bought one, and it is a pleasure to be able to hear the birds singing while you mow the lawn.

www.gardenorganic.org.uk

This site, for organic gardeners and those who dream of being one, is also the site for the Henry Doubleday Research Association (HDRA), which is dedicated to the working pleasures and encouragement of organic gardening. Here you can find somewhere to have **a great day out**, all the **information** you need to get started, and **what to do in your garden now,** as well as **organic gardens for schools** and a **catalogue**. Become a **member**, and there's even more.

www.greengardener.co.uk

Everything for the 'green' garden: biological pest controls, wormeries and water butts, ladybirds, homes for your wild companions, lawn fertilizers, and answers to your questions.

www.omlet.co.uk/homepage/homepage.php

Anyone with a town garden who wants to keep chickens should visit this site. The eglu is the perfect home for your organically raised egg-laying pets, or a rabbit or guinea pig if you'd prefer.

www.organicgarden.org.uk

This is a good site for anyone starting to garden organically either in the back garden or on an allotment. **Start here** is where the garden begins, **garden tour** shows how it can grow, and **growing** has the resources to help it flourish. There is also a **forum** and many excellent links.

www.passionflow.co.uk/index.htm

Anyone passionate about *passifloras* will love this site.

www.rspb.org.uk/gardens

Advice from the Royal Society for the Protection of Birds to encourage birds and butterflies into your garden, and to get rid of the slugs in non-toxic ways.

www.theseedsite.co.uk

Everything you could possibly want to know about seeds, from how they look to how to collect them, plant them and then harvest them for the next year.

www.wigglywigglers.co.uk

Wiggly Wigglers, a gardening company from Herefordshire that encourages nature back into the garden, won the Federation of Small Businesses Champions Award in 2005. Everything you need to create a healthy wildlife garden is available here: worm farms to turn food scraps into compost; beehive-like composters that come in ten colours; and the Bokashi, a revolutionary composter that uses micro-organisms to break down all food waste, including meat and fish scraps, in a bin no bigger than a small kitchen rubbish bin. Pest control includes **bugboxes** to give ladybirds and lacewings, which eat aphids, a winter home; and **slug**-eating nematodes. **Wildflowers** shows their wide selection of native grasses, flowers and hedging, all of which are essential for the well-being and survival of indigenous birds and insects. There are packs for building a wildlife **pond**, and bouquets of **flowers**, fresh from their gardens to any address in the UK.

www.wildlife-gardening.co.uk

Wildlife-gardening advice from Jenny Steel, an experienced creator of gardens that encourage wildlife and help maintain the biodiversity of our native species.

GIFTS

....

www.climatecare.org/calculators/gift_offsets.cfm
Give the gift of a healthier planet to a loved one by offsetting some of their CO_2.

www.goodgifts.org
Good Gifts offers inspirational choices for presents that will satisfy even the most hard-to-please member of the family. You can buy a tank that will give five blacksmiths a year's work as they break it down into farming tools for local families – swords into ploughshares. Or you can buy a hive of bees, give someone the gift of sight, give a bike to a midwife, or provide heart surgery for a baby, a chilli hedge to keep elephants off the garden, or reading lessons for a mother.

www.heifer.org
The Heifer Project believes that by donating animals to people in need, you can help them feed themselves, and through sustainable farming, help them produce more animals to feed their community. If you're looking for a special gift, explore this site. I've purchased many Christmas presents here.

www.oxfamunwrapped.com
Here are wedding gifts with a difference. Through your generosity, the lives of many can be changed. You fill in **wedding-list** as usual, but instead of giving plates, glasses, frying-pans and the ubiquitous toaster, your guests can buy you goats, beehives, a mango plantation, donkeys, trees, irrigation, the provision of safe water, a

month's worth of teaching, even a camel, which are then sent as gifts to families living in poverty elsewhere in the world. Not getting married? You can create a **wish-list** for yourself that you can send to anyone who asks, 'What do you want for your birthday?' And **corporate gift**-givers can find alternatives to those bags full of useless goodies.

GLOBAL WARMING

SEE ALSO: Action, Bicycles, Cars, Climate Change, Educate Yourself, Energy, Films, Hydrogen Fuel Cells, Lighting, Nuclear, Transportation

The Earth is heating up. By burning fossil fuels, humans are adding carbon dioxide and other heat-trapping greenhouse gases to the atmosphere at what may be a perilous rate. We are exacerbating the problem by cutting down the very forests that could help to absorb our excess carbon dioxide. The consequences of global warming are potentially catastrophic, but you can help change the situation.

www.climatestar.org
The causes of global warming, its impact and the solutions.

www.numberwatch.co.uk/warmlist.htm
This extensive database of articles listing the effects of global warming on the Earth and its inhabitants is very persuasive.

www.treeflights.com
Air travel is a major contributor to global warming because of the amount of carbon dioxide produced by aircraft. If you are a frequent flyer, one way of helping to abate that CO_2 is to plant trees that will absorb it and turn it into wood. On this site you can contribute to the planting of trees in a Welsh forest each time you fly. It will not make your flight completely carbon neutral, but it will be a step in the right direction.

www.undoit.org/undoit_steps_1.cfm
Take Environmental Defense's twenty simple steps and help undo global warming.

GOLF

....

Golf courses traditionally consume masses of fresh water, and need huge amounts of fertilizers and pesticides to keep them 'healthy'. The subsequent run-off pollutes groundwater, streams, rivers and lakes. Now some in the golf industry are working to reverse the environmental blight of these worldwide playgrounds.

....

www.golfenvironmenteurope.org
Golf Environment Europe is committed to the environmental improvement of golf courses through conservation of biodiversity and water, energy efficiency, minimizing waste and the sustainable development of new courses.

GREEN ROOFS

....

SEE ALSO: **Architecture, Eden Project, Sustainable Living**

Growing a garden on your roof is a great idea for those of us who have access to a flat roof, and not much garden at ground level. However, a roof garden has a lot more to offer than just a pleasant place to sit out on a hot night. Roofs covered in grass, plants and small trees are springing up in cities all over the world. They keep your home cool by absorbing ultraviolet radiation, they provide extra sound and temperature insulation, they make the air you breathe cleaner, they soak up rainwater that would otherwise add to storm-water run-off, and they provide an essential habitat for wildlife. Huge flat roofs can be enjoyed as parks and public recreation areas.

....

www.greenroofs.com
A resource portal for anyone interested in green roofs.

www.livingroofs.org
Click on **benefits** to discover why a roof garden would be good for you and your property; find answers to your questions in **perceived barriers**; and see what can be done in **case studies**.

PEOPLE WHO DID

Dusty Gedge looks at flat roofs and sees potential habitats for the myriad species that are being threatened with habitat loss through urban redevelopment. This passion was born when, as a volunteer for the London Biodiversity Partnership, he observed that urban wastelands of brick, concrete and rubble were teeming with life, including many rare invertebrates, and his particular favourite, the black redstart, one of Britain's rarest birds. However, because these same urban wastelands were rapidly being developed, hopes of protecting these creatures were not looking good, until the day Dusty looked up and saw the potential of flat roofs. He realized that on their level, heat-baked, dry surfaces it would be possible to re-create the same arid habitat as rubble-strewn ground, and thus save the black redstart and its cohabitants. But how to achieve that dream? He had spent much of his life watching birds – now he wanted to give something back to them. A plane ride to Switzerland connected him with Stephan Brenneisen, an expert on green roofs, who confirmed that Dusty was on the right track.

Back in London, he began working with the idea of using scrap brick and concrete as the substrate for his living roofs (thus keeping it out of landfill), and he started to persuade a number of London property owners to let him create the rooftop brownfield-like sites that he hoped would attract the black redstart, and be naturally colonized by many other species. He co-founded Livingroofs.org as a resource for those interested in building a green roof. The fact that he has designed living roofs for many buildings in Canary Wharf, Deptford and elsewhere in London is a sign of his success, and in 2004 he was given the Andrew Lees Memorial Award, the British Environment and Media's top prize, for that achievement. Barclays Bank put the world's highest living roof – specifically designed to encourage local biodiversity – on their new worldwide headquarters in Canary Wharf. Through this there is a growing interest in green roofs designed specifically for nature conservation.

Dusty's passion continues. 'Vast areas of London's roofs could be greened. You could have house sparrows, bats, wetlands, anything you want, but the key is to link them to local nature conservation and not import landscape conceits,' he has said. Air quality would improve, wildlife would flourish, buildings would be better insulated, and the storm-water run-off problem would be ameliorated. Not a bad achievement for someone who describes himself as 'a geezer from Deptford'. Dusty is a trailblazer, but he believes that living sustainably means you are part of a community, and that without the support of the many people who have been part of his movement, he wouldn't have succeeded.

H

HEALTH

See also: Children, Cleaning Products, Home, Pesticides and Toxins, Plastic and Alternatives, Smoking

http://database.healthandenvironment.org
The Collaborative on Health and the Environment's searchable database has information summarizing the links between chemical toxins and human diseases as well as other conditions. **Science** takes you further.

www.drgreene.com
In December 1995, Dr Alan Greene, a American paediatrician, started this website as a way of communicating widely with parents about the common issues of raising children: feeding and teething problems, toilet training, sleeping difficulties, and the interconnection between a healthy environment and a healthy child. Parents from all over the world can communicate directly with Dr Greene by clicking on **chat schedule** to ask him a question in real time. **Answers** has an encyclopaedic listing of information under **topic centres**, covering every aspect of family health.

www.ewg.org/reports/skindeep
Use this Environmental Working Group's cosmetic safety list to assess the safety of the ingredients in your regular skin and hair products.

www.healthyflooring.org
Many of the flooring materials in our buildings can be unhealthy. Click on **information** for **the guide to healthy flooring** to learn about the allergens and toxins, such as **PVC**, being used, **what you can do at home** to reduce the impact of those allergens and **contaminants**, and what the **alternatives** might be. There is also a list of **alternative flooring suppliers**.

www.ourstolenfuture.org
The book *Our Stolen Future* drew the world's attention to the serious problems that some manufactured chemicals can cause to developing foetuses. Scientific studies show that these endocrine disrupters are affecting both humans and wildlife. This site introduces you to the ideas discussed in the book, helps you to understand those ideas, connects you to the most up-to-date information, and offers suggestions about what you as a consumer can do to minimize the risk of exposure to these hormonally disruptive contaminants.

www.psr.org
Winner of the 1985 Nobel Prize for Peace, Physicians for Social Responsibility brings together citizens and physicians to fight for public policies that protect human health and safety. Click on **environment and health**, where **international** connects you to the International

Society of Doctors for the Environment. Once there, **links** connects you to groups actively promoting better health for all.

www.silentspring.org

A partnership of scientists, doctors, public-health advocates and community activists, which works to identify – and then change – the ways in which pollution and the environment impact upon women's health. They are especially concerned with breast cancer.

www.wwf.org.uk/chemicals/home.asp

WWF's **chemicals in the home** is part of their **chemicals and health** campaign. You will find lists of what to avoid and what to use, and an excellent glossary, links to the **latest research**, ten **top tips** to avoid exposure to chemicals, and a link to the **safer shopping** site. **Blood testing** has information on surveys WWF have done to test the amount of contamination in people from these persistent toxins. Take the **quiz** in **indecent exposure**, and then take action to remove these hazardous substances from your world.

HOME

www.greenmoves.com

Green Moves is an advertising service for energy-efficient, 'green' homes, so if you are interested in buying one (or selling yours and building another one), this is the site for you. **Environmental features** lists the characteristics of the houses they accept, and **how to advertise** has the information necessary to do just that.

www.greenscore.org.uk

Use this site to check how green you and your household are. When the result is in, **global action plan** offers some practical tips to improve your score and save you money.

www.greenshop.co.uk

'Environmental products for a sustainable future' are sold in the real shop at Bisley near Stroud, or online from this site. **About us** introduces you to the history and philosophy of the Green Shop, and there are links to the **solar** and **rainwater** parts of the business, as well as many other items useful for sustainable living, including a **log maker** that recycles newspapers into logs for the fire, and garden furniture made from old ox-cart wheels and other disused farming tools. There are compact fluorescent light bulbs under **energy** and a lot to explore under **links**.

www.gwll.org.uk

This information source for green living in Leicestershire is relevant to the whole country. Every category in this site is excellent, starting with the vision, 'A world where actively caring for the environment is second nature.' **Our projects** is packed full of great ideas, including **the green doctor,** who can come to your home and advise you on what you can do to be greener; there's **allotments for all**; you can donate that old bike to **bikes 4 all**, where it will be repaired and made available to someone who needs it; join **green accounts** and get paid for recycling (which could help the pocket-money fund); recycle your old mobile phone; and when you've done all that, take a stroll in the **Orchards local nature reserve**.

www.naturalcollection.com

Natural Goods won the *Observer*'s Ethical Retailer of the Year in 2006. The principles of Fairtrade, sustainability and the power of the consumer to affect the way goods are made are the bedrock of this online store for household products. Read how these principles are implemented in **about us**, use the **dot guides** for even more information, and then explore the huge range of beautiful, practical, eco-friendly goods on offer. This site proves that living green does not mean living dull.

www.safer-products.org

On 22 March 2005, a report entitled *Sick of Dust: Chemicals in Common Products – a Needless Health Threat in our Homes* was published in the United States. Samples of dust from seventy homes around the country had been analysed in the autumn of 2004, and the results showed that every one contained all the hazardous persistent chemicals that were being tested for: alkylphenols, brominated flame-retardants, organotins, perfluorinated chemicals, pesticides and phthalates. Every one of these chemicals is suspected of causing cancer, allergies and immune-system damage, as well as being linked to hormone disruption, which can in turn cause reproductive and developmental problems. Household products should not contain contaminating chemicals that can adversely affect our environment and us. There are other options, based on green chemistry principles. Consumers must become more aware of the issue and begin pressuring for change. Start here. **Resources/links** has much to offer. Download the **dust report**, read it and give copies to everyone in your community. Learn where the dangers lie, find out which companies are already using healthier materials in their products and support them. If safer products are unavailable, start asking that they be made available. This is something that affects us all.

www.warrenevans.com
Beds and other furniture made in London in a socially responsible manner by local craftsmen, using environmentally friendly timber. When I lived in London, I had a Warren Evans bed, and I loved it.

theyellowhouse.org.uk/index.html
The story of how a 1930s council house was remodelled into an eco-friendly, energy-saving home.

HYDROGEN FUEL CELLS

SEE ALSO: **Peak Oil**

We will run out of fossil fuels sooner than we think. Hydrogen fuel, produced by wind, solar, hydro and biomass power, could be the energy of the future. It is made from water and, when burned, becomes water again, which some experts say you can drink. That's clean!

www.fuelcells.org
The Online Fuel Cell Information Resource is a good introduction to fuel-cell technology.

www.fuelcellstoday.com
A global fuel-cell portal. To expand your knowledge of this technology, click on **reference** and then **education kit**.

www.hydrogen.org.au
The website for the National Hydrogen Association of Australia, winner of the 2004 Macarthur Environment Award, has links to information about hydrogen-fuel-cell technology and other intriguing things.

www.rmi.org/sitepages/pid171.php#20H2Myths
Twenty hydrogen myths explored and debunked by Amory Lovins of the Rocky Mountain Institute.

www.tfl.gov.uk/buses/fuel-cell-buses.asp
Check out the hydrogen-fuel-cell buses being tested in London, download the schedule and take a ride.

I

INVESTMENT

See also: Natural Laws

Socially Responsible Investment (SRI) is the commitment to invest in companies, products and services that are economically, environmentally and socially responsible. If you are concerned about the well-being of life on Earth, and you have investments, then a powerful way to help promote sustainability is to invest responsibly.

www.co-operativebank.co.uk
Click on **ethics in action,** then **ecology** and find out how the Co-operative Bank's commitment to sustainability has influenced the choices they are making.

www.eiris.org
Ethical Investment Research Services uses its extensive resources to comprehensively research the environmental and ethical responsibility of companies, in order to help their clients make investment decisions that will match their principles. This site is an excellent tool for anyone interested in socially and environmentally responsible investments. Click on **personal finance** to find an adviser, and start from there. Students and teachers will find material for their research under **academics**. There is information for **companies**, and

under **charities** there is a **toolkit** with guidelines for responsible investment.

www.greenmoneyjournal.com
A journal for those interested in socially responsible investing.

www.triodos.co.uk
Use your savings to help the environment with the Triodos Bank. Through Triodos you can target your savings to fund organic farms, Fairtrade companies, wind projects, clean-water schemes, reuse of waste, and many other ethical investments. Click on **savings** in **who we finance** and see what your money could be doing.

J

JOBS

Many of the sites in this book offer employment opportunities.

www.ethical-jobs.co.uk

If you are interested in working for a charity, in the environmental arena, for an NGO, in the field of social work or volunteering, then you might find the perfect job listed here.

JUNK MAIL

Junk mail is the most annoying aspect of having a letterbox. Every year, millions of tons of this waste paper end up in landfill. That's thousands of rubbish trucks filled with nothing but junk mail! Put up a sign saying 'No Junk Mail'.

www.mpsonline.org.uk/mpsr

Scroll down to the bottom of the page, click on **register** and remove junk mail from your life – and the paper-recycling bin.

www.junk-mail.org.uk

Use the tools on this site to remove junk mail from your letterbox permanently.

K

KEEP UK BEAUTIFUL

SEE ALSO: **National Parks, Walking**

---

www.aonb.org.uk
The gateway to Areas of Outstanding Natural Beauty (AONB) in England, Wales and Northern Ireland. This designation indicates that the landscape in question is so beautiful and discrete that it is a national treasure, and must be treated as such.

www.beautifulbritain.co.uk
Out and about has destination beauty spots. **Wildlife** is full of pleasures, including instructions for building a **wildlife pond**, humane **mouse** traps, and a series of enchanting photographs from a camera in a blue tit's nest box. If you want to do the same, click on **bird boxes** to learn how to build one, then **installing a nest box camera**, and start photographing. There are downloadable desktop **jigsaws** for PC users.

www.ccw.gov.uk
The Countryside Council for Wales takes care of the wild beauty of Wales. **Our work** leads to **habitats and species**, where you will discover that wildlife isn't just what you see in exotic places on the TV, it's also there **on your doorstep**. Download a **list of plants that attract wildlife**

and see who comes calling. **Places to visit** has **reserves** and **trails** to wander round and enjoy.

www.encams.org

Keep Britain Tidy runs many **campaigns** to achieve the goal of cleaner streets and beaches throughout the UK.

www.england-in-particular.info

Enter the gateway to this intriguing site and you will encounter the mythology, ecology, orchards, architecture, landscape, history and eternal beauty of Britain. Follow the paths as they lead you through woods, along rivers, past the green man or the white horse, and revel in our collective common ground.

www.english-nature.org.uk

English Nature's focus is the protection and conservation of the environment for future generations. **Springwatch with Bill Oddie** has many PDFs to help you create a wildlife haven in your garden, and if you click on **wildlife and geology** and then **nature in your garden** there is even more. There are **spotlight reserves** to explore under **NNRs** in **special sites** – the principal wildlife habitat areas and geological formations in Britain. **Walks and events** lists local activities you could join, to enjoy being part of the natural world.

www.mournelive.com/index.asp

The mountains of Mourne in Northern Ireland have been designated an Area of Outstanding Natural Beauty since 1966. Visitors can enjoy mountains, beaches, farmed drumlin and hill country, ancient monuments and castles. **Out and about** has places to **walk**, places to **cycle**, places to **stay**, and things to do in the summer. **Biodiversity**, and

key habitats and **species** are covered in **natural heritage**. Locals interested in volunteering can find out **how to get involved**. The **interactive map** is like a guidebook to help you plan your trip, and **virtual tours** shows you the panoramic view.

www.snh.org.uk

The Scottish Natural Heritage site celebrates the biodiversity of this beautiful land. Your comments and suggestions are welcomed. **Learn about** connects you to the diverse habitats that make up Scotland, the species living in those habitats, the geology underlying them, and what you might find in your own area.

L

LAUNDRY
....

SEE ALSO: Cleaning Products, Dry-cleaning, Home

To save energy and lower your electricity bill, consider the following: wash your laundry at the lowest possible recommended temperature, even cold. Don't waste water and energy by washing lots of small loads.Use a clothes line for drying wherever possible. To extend your machine's life and functionability, run it empty every two to three months on a warm cycle, using white vinegar instead of detergent.

....

www.ecover.com/gb/en/default_home.aspx
You'll find Ecover's laundry products in the **utility room**. They contain no optical brighteners (chemicals that make your clothes look brighter than they really are), many of their ingredients are plant-based, and they are not harmful to you or the aquatic life they might encounter after they leave your washing machine.

www.shopeco.co.uk
Click on **soapnuts** for products that will wash your clothes without using any harsh or polluting detergents. My sister uses soapnuts for her wash and loves them. I have a friend who swears by ecoballs , which can last for one thousand washes, and there are dryer balls that can reduce your drying time by a quarter.

LIGHTING

SEE ALSO: **Business, Energy, Reduce-Reuse-Recycle**

A compact fluorescent light bulb (CFL) will last up to thirteen times longer than an incandescent bulb and uses 75 per cent less electricity to produce the same light. Thus, the light output from a 25-watt CFL equals that from a 100-watt incandescent bulb, which actually produces more heat than light. CFL bulbs cost more to buy, but provide major savings in the long term. Follow the example of the Marriott hotel chain in the USA, which saved millions by switching to CFLs – replace your most-used light bulbs with CFLs.

www.banthebulb.org

Matt Prescott runs this information-packed blog dedicated to his campaign to replace incandescent bulbs with energy-efficient ones. There are extensive links to advice, suppliers of cheap CFLs, savings, the history of the light bulb, renewable energy, commentary, other environmental bloggers and more. Who knew that a light bulb could engender such passion? But passion is what we need in this drive to change the way we live.

www.efficientlight.co.uk

Learn the facts about energy-saving bulbs and then place your order.

www.sunpipe.co.uk

Sunpipes bring the sunlight into areas that normally need artificial light during the day. That's light you don't need to pay for. Monodraught offers a wide range of sunpipes that will light any space during daylight hours, from a small bathroom to a large ballroom. Click on **the sunflower** to see what's available and how it works. **Solavent** combines a sunpipe with solar-powered ventilation and two compact fluorescent downlighters, perfect for a bathroom or for over the stove. **Design** has ways to light the basement, and for installing sunpipes on to a turf roof; **FAQs** has a forty-page booklet with the answers to your questions; you can **download** brochures and technical details; and the ten-step ordering process in **buy online** is easy to follow.

LOCAL GOVERNMENT

Sustainable practices begin at home, and local governing bodies can provide the tools to help their citizens achieve a way of living that will be healthier for them and the country.

www.direct.gov.uk/homepage/fs/en

To find your local council's website, click on **directories**, then **local councils**. Use this to find out about hazardous-waste services, recycling collections, and the many other choices provided to help you keep stuff out of landfill.

PEOPLE WHO DID

WHEN **Matt Prescott** was six, he would watch the squirrels in his garden and wonder where they went and what they did when he couldn't see them. His interest in nature led him to study Zoology at university, and while there, he set up a recycling scheme for students. which he hoped would become a model for a city-wide recycling service. To that end, he persuaded the student union to provide a minibus and driver, the city council to supply the bins, He got the student newspaper to publicize the service, co-opted students to run it, and found a local charity to recycle the collected waste. The result was that many people became accustomed to the value and habit of recycling, which in turn led to the council improving their waste collection and recycling service. Through that experience, Matt realized not only that he was capable of finding a solution to a problem, but also that he could bring out the best in others while they helped him implement the solution.

After completing his undergraduate degree, Matt found himself in Uganda on a training course for young ecologists. His experiences there, and subsequently in the slums of Kenya, awakened in him a strong desire to use his education to find practical solutions to the enormous global environmental problems that he was witnessing on a daily basis.

Back at Oxford to work on a Ph.D., he started inviting leaders in the environmental world to talk to students and created a very active blog (www.earth-info.net), but became quickly over-run by the demands of all that he was trying to achieve. So he decided to focus on one single issue, and chose energy efficiency and the banning of incandescent light bulbs, because he feels that the role of energy efficiency in the fight to stop global warming is something that is being overlooked by the general public, even though it is something they could easily incorporate into their daily lives. After all, energy-efficient bulbs have been available for a long time, and yet they are still not the major market sector that they should be. Matt's aim is for us all to limit the effects of global warming by replacing our incandescent bulbs with energy-efficient bulbs. Following the publication of the recent Energy Review in the UK, Tony Blair indicated that he would be asking the EU to ban incandescent light bulbs, which indicates that Matt might be successful in his campaign.

LONDON

SEE ALSO: Birds, Children, Design, Gardens, Home, Hydrogen Fuel Cells, Local Government, Reduce-Reuse-Recycle, Sustainable Living, Waste

www.capitalwastefacts.com
The one-stop site for information on recycling and waste in London.

www.greenchain.com
The Green Chain is a forty-mile network of footpaths through south-east London that begins on the Thames at Thamesmead, Erith or the Thames Barrier, wanders through historic parks, local villages, ancient woodlands and meadows, and ends up at Crystal Palace. You can choose walks for children, circular walks, or linear walks that are linked to bus services to get you back home. Click on **5 great days out on the green chain** and choose where to go and what to see.

www.infolondon.ukf.net/organic
This directory will help you find organic food in London.

www.lcc.org.uk
The London Cycling Campaign's mission is for London to be a great city for cyclists. If you want to be in on the ride, everything you will need is here – bike-shop discounts, free maps, advice, insurance and a comprehensive **guide** to a healthy life.

www.lfm.org.uk

A list of London Farmers' Markets with the **maps** to help you find them.

www.londonremade.com

London Remade is all about recycling in London. They say that up to 80 per cent of London's household rubbish should be recycled, so click on any of the links on the opening page and you will be connected to a wealth of information that will help you do that. **Business support** has programmes to help with the establishment of small recycling businesses, or the **inspired recycling** of waste into desirable things. **Making recycled products** links you to many of the eco-processing sites being developed that are closing **the loop** of London's rubbish.

www.lsx.org.uk

The London Sustainability Exchange is an information service for Londoners wanting to put green practices at the centre of everything they do. **Who's who** lists those already doing it, and you can add your eco-friendly group or business if they aren't already there. The **Green Start services guide**, under **sustainability and lifelong learning**, has information about green products and services for nurseries and childcare centres. **Sustainability at work and home** has guides for greening the home, the office, meetings and seminars. But these are just scratching the surface. There is much to explore in this dense site, for planners, business people and householders who are seeking to make London a great, sustainable city.

www.realisenetwork.co.uk

If you want to get rid of some stuff, but don't want to clutter up landfill, this site could be very useful. Realise Network's database will connect you to services that will recycle/reuse that stuff. There is also information about goods made from recycled materials. Businesses and individuals can get rid of IT goods, and those interested in buying such goods can find sources here.

www.streetcar.co.uk

Streetcar offers you the opportunity to drive a car, but not own it. Their VW Golfs are parked all over London, and when you need a car, you book it online or by phone, find the car at a location near you, unlock it with your card, type your pin into the dashboard and off you go. Membership is free and **user guide** has all the information. Businesses interested in this service should click on **for organisations**.

www.tfl.gov.uk/tfl

Use Transport for London to help you get around without using a car.

M

MEAT

See also: Action, Educate Yourself, Farming, Food, Films

www.ciwf.org.uk/eatlessmeat
The industrial production of meat, eggs and dairy products is giving rise to serious problems with human health, environmental health and, last but not least, the health and well-being of the animals in the production line. Eating less meat is one answer – if we eat less, there will be less demand and therefore less need for factory farms.

Why? lays out the reasons, **how?** suggests alternative choices, with recipes and where to buy the ingredients, and **kids only** has suggestions for the lunchbox.

www.seedsofhealth.co.uk/resources/meat/index.shtml
A list of UK producers of grass-fed and organic meat.

MEETINGS AND GATHERINGS

SEE ALSO: Community, Eden Project, Sustainable Living

www.bluegreenmeetings.org
BlueGreen Meetings offers ideas to hosts, planners and suppliers who want their gatherings to be environmentally responsible.

www.edenproject.com/visiting/1868.html
One of the most exciting places in the world to hold an event is the visionary Eden Project in Cornwall. The details are here.

www.environ.org.uk/ecohouse/meeting_room/index.php
Have your meeting at the EcoHouse in Leicester.

MOBILE PHONES

SEE ALSO: Batteries, Local Councils, Office, Reduce-Reuse-Recycle, Sustainable Living, Trees

Whenever you buy a new mobile phone, the question is what happens to the one being discarded. The one place it shouldn't end up in is the dump. Mobile phones and their accessories contain some of the most poisonous substances known to us: cadmium, lead, nickel, mercury, manganese, lithium, zinc, arsenic, antimony, beryllium and copper. These toxins eventually leach out of landfill into the soil and water, and from there they enter the food chain.

You could end up eating your mobile phone, which would not be good for your health. A wide range of problems, from the nervous system and reproductive health to developmental abnormalities and cancer can come from these chemicals. So what can you do? Check the website of your local council for recycling and hazardous-waste information. Maybe the manufacturer of your ex-mobile phone has a suggestion, as some are now collecting old batteries and phones for safe disposal. Or maybe you could give it to a friend, or one of the many charities that collect them.

---

www.recyclemymobile.co.uk

Recycle your old mobile phone for cash.

www.envirofone.com

Trade in your mobile phone, get cash or credit with Argos, and a donation made to charity on your behalf.

N

NAPPIES

SEE ALSO: Children, Environment, London

'Eight million nappies are thrown away in Britain every day – nearly three billion every year.' Green Services Guide for Childcare Centres in London

According to research, a disposable nappy can take up to five hundred years to decompose in landfill, which means that every disposable nappy thrown away still exists. It is certainly convenient to use disposable nappies, but the price to the environment is high. Cloth nappies have been shown to be less expensive both for the family budget and for the Earth. There is some concern that the washing of cloth nappies would stress a seriously challenged water supply, but the Women's Environmental Network has stated that if you take into account the amount of water used in the manufacture of disposables, it is two and a half times the amount used to make and wash a cloth nappy. However you cut it, disposables are the more unsustainable choice.

www.babykind.co.uk/whatwillineed.htm
This site offers a wealth of information to anyone wanting to use cloth nappies – from cost to type, style, fitting and laundering.

www.changeanappy.co.uk
Click on **information** and you will see why the service offered by the National Association of Nappy Services is the right choice for hospitals, childcare services and busy parents, when it comes to changing baby. **Find a supplier** can connect you to a weekly service that provides clean cotton nappies and the collection of soiled ones at a price that is comparable, or even less, than the real cost of disposables – if you take into account the environmental cost of producing and disposing of them, as well as what you pay when you buy them.

www.cottonbottoms.co.uk
Healthy cotton nappies. Learn how to fold one in **wash at home**, which also links you to reports on the levels of the oestrogen-mimic TBT hormone being found in disposables.

www.wen.org.uk/nappies/facts.htm
Nappy facts from the Women's Environmental Network.

NATIONAL PARKS

www.dartmoor-npa.gov.uk
Apart from all the usual pleasures of Dartmoor, the National Park Authority offers the **Dartmoor freewheeler**, a free bus that takes you and your bike up on to the moor so you can freewheel all the way down. Or there are **guided walks** for those who like to know about where they are going.

www.mylinkspage.com/natpark.html#AON
An extensive list of websites covering all aspects of National Parks and Areas of Outstanding Natural Beauty (AONBs), including campaigns to conserve and protect areas that you might want to get involved with. Websites connected to these issues can be linked to this page.

www.nationalparks.gov.uk
Britain has fourteen National Parks, and this site connects you to them all. Each one is different and, as growing numbers of us live in crowded cities, each offers us the opportunity to experience the natural world away from the noise and rush of urban living. They also provide essential habitats for rare native species, and **looking after** introduces ongoing conservation projects. National Parks are havens for all, and we should ensure their survival by getting to know them and supporting them.

NATURAL LAWS

SEE ALSO: **Architecture, Sustainable Living, Water**

If we are going to live sustainably, we need to begin to recognize the fundamental importance of natural laws. These are the physical laws that control Earth's living systems, and for too long they have been ignored by the economic systems that run our lives. Consequently, we now face the serious possibility of a collapsing global environment. To live sustainably we must start living within the means that the Earth provides, not beyond them. Businesses all over the world are beginning to understand that the bottom line is healthier if it is achieved in

*partnership with these laws, and those that continue old
practices will fall by the wayside.*

Natural laws include such simple truths as these:

⮕ To have a future, living things must live sustainably,
producing only products that can be utilized by some
other organism or broken down into inert
components.

⮕ No species living in a closed system can continue to
expand its population indefinitely. Earth receives
energy from the sun, but is otherwise a closed
system.

⮕ In order to survive, all species require some degree
of stability in their habitat.

⮕ The lives of every species, including humans, depend
directly or indirectly on the lives of other species.

⮕ All life, including human life, is a product of evolution
and therefore selfish by its nature. Selfish behaviour
is an advantage to species until they dominate their
closed system entirely, whereupon it becomes a fatal
disadvantage – always.

*Just for the record: we in the developed world are
currently out of step with every one of the above natural laws.*

....

www.cleanproduction.org

This is one of my favourite sites, because it demonstrates
that humanity's worst problems are solvable, most
solutions are simple, and existing scientific knowledge is
sufficient for us to implement those solutions. This
international consortium of community groups,
environmental organizations, public-health advocates

and trade unions is pressurizing industry to start using green technologies that can remove poisonous, hazardous chemicals from our lives. **Steps to clean production** will take you to the heart of the matter. **BioSociety** has a story about a **zero-waste brewery** that produces 800,000 litres of beer annually and uses its waste to produce mushrooms, chickens, eggs, fish, flowers, rye, tomatoes and energy. Other links in **steps** explain the **precautionary principle**, the **closed-loop system** and **sustainable consumption**, all principles of this new industrial revolution, a revolution that we should be challenging our industries to join.

www.forumforthefuture.org.uk

Forum for the Future employs science-based, practical tools to help businesses, government bodies and others to adopt sustainable practices that will improve their future as well as that of the Earth. Zero waste, closed-loop production systems, social justice and the management of key natural resources are their chief concerns. **Business** leads to **the natural step**. Download the **natural step framework** pdf to learn more.

www.zeri.org

'Don't expect the Earth to produce more. Expect humans to do more with what the Earth produces. This is the second Green revolution.' Gunter Pauli.

Zero Emissions Research and Initiatives (ZERI), founded by environmental entrepreneur Gunter Pauli, is a global network of creative minds that view waste as a resource. By using solutions based on science and natural laws, they are altering the normal paradigms of 'business as usual' and bringing economic health to impoverished communities all over the world. Pauli calls it Upsizing. **About Zeri** explains how it works. **Case**

studies has inspirational examples of the more than fifty projects ZERI is currently working with, **science** introduces the basis of the process, and **education** has the tools with which Pauli and his team are introducing their **vision** to future generations.

NEWS

Subscribe to online newsletters – many of the sites in this book have one – and save money, paper and energy while investigating ideas and resources to help you make informed choices. Many magazines and newspapers also offer this option.

www.enn.com

Use the Environmental News Network's free daily bulletins to stay abreast of environmental issues.

www.EnvironmentalHealthNews.org

The daily publication of Environmental Health Sciences – a US organization that helps the public understand the science behind environmental exposures and human health.

www.greenfutures.org.uk

Green Futures is a magazine for those interested in sustainable solutions. The magazine provides cutting-edge, entertaining commentary on such issues as sustainable business and what that really means, environmental choices that are socially beneficial, eco-logical footprints, natural capitalism and other hot topics. Subscribers can access articles as far back as 2000.

www.gristmagazine.com
Environmental commentary from the USA, where many are concerned at the size of their country's environmental footprint.

www.newscientist.com/home.ns
Keep abreast of the latest news in the fascinating realms of science and the natural world through the journal *New Scientist*. There are articles on everything from the effects of climate change on the oceans, to the latest breakthroughs in technology, to understanding how we humans work, and what's happening in outer space.

www.oriononline.org
'America's finest environmental magazine' (*Boston Globe*) features articles by some of the country's leading thinkers and writers.

www.peopleandplanet.net/doc.php?id=2652
If you are curious as to whether the ethics of living green are entering the mainstream, read this article about the Ethical Consumerism Report of 2004.

www.resurgence.org
Resurgence magazine connects you to a world of 'ecology, art and culture'. Sample a selection of its features from past issues by some of our most exceptional writers and thinkers on ecological and spiritual matters. Join a **readers' group** and share ideas over a seasonal meal, or mingle with the online community in **Gaia's café**.

www.theecologist.org/home.asp
The *Ecologist* is read widely around the world, and has

been central to many international environmental campaigns. If you want to know the story behind the story, and how deeply the connections run, this magazine will help you understand the complexity of the environmental issues that swirl around us daily. **Find your local box scheme** will link you to all the local suppliers in the country selling locally produced food. Sign on to their **eco power campaign** and buy your electricity from local, renewable resources. **Act!** will help you start to make a difference. **Daily life** has many articles about everyday matters and **behind the label** may make you rethink your shopping habits.

www.treehugger.com

A popular international web magazine offering reviews, comment, news and recommendations for green products.

NUCLEAR

Nuclear power carries with it serious safety concerns, and ongoing problems about how to dispose safely of the waste, which remains toxic for thousands of years, and the fact that the process of uranium mining is very polluting. It is not the clean, green energy source that some are proclaiming it to be.

www.kiddofspeed.com

The daughter of a Russian nuclear physicist, Elena is passionate about motorcycles – she rides a Kawasaki ZZR-1100. She was a schoolgirl in 1986 when the reactor of the nuclear-power plant at Chernobyl exploded in the early hours of 26 April, creating one of the most toxic places on Earth and spreading radiation for thousands of miles across Europe. It may be nine hundred years before anyone can live safely in Chernobyl and the surrounding region again. Through the influence of her father, Elena obtained a pass to travel on her motorcycle into the silent, empty world of Chernobyl. Her photo journal is extraordinary in its simplicity as she observes the devastating effects of the explosion. Forty-eight thousand people had to abandon absolutely everything, even the clothes they stood up in, and walk away from their lives, never to return. Elena's record of this human tragedy forces us to recognize the danger of living with nuclear power.

www.foe.co.uk/resource/faqs/questions/nuclear_energy.html
Friends of the Earth answers the question, 'Is nuclear power the answer to our energy needs?'

www.nirs.org/climate/climate.htm
The Nuclear Information and Resource Service addresses the question of the amelioration of climate change by the use of nuclear power. Read the recent talk given by Mary Olsen to the UN Commission on Sustainable Development – **A False Myth of Nuclear Power: Nuclear Power Expansion Is No Remedy for Climate Change**'.

www.wagingpeace.org
The Nuclear Age Peace Foundation's mission is to abolish nuclear weapons worldwide, and to use peace as a means of creating a safer world for us, for our children, and for our children's children. Click on **issues** to learn about the dangers of nuclear energy, nuclear waste and nuclear weapons.

O

OCEANS

....

SEE ALSO: Action, Conservation, Coral Reefs, Educate Yourself, Fish, Schools, Surfing, Teachers, Tourism, Volunteering

Oceans cover 71 per cent of the Earth's surface and therefore seem infinitely able to support all we can remove from them or dump into them. But that is a misconception, and it is becoming increasingly clear that the worldwide depletion of fish stocks, coastal overdevelopment, increasing pollution from cities, industrial processes and agriculture, and the effects of global warming are causing ocean ecosystems to collapse.

....

www.greenpeace.org.uk/oceans

Greenpeace's ocean pages give an excellent overview of the health of the oceans and the creatures that live within them, which are introduced in the **species guide** and **slideshow**. The problem of over-fishing is covered extensively, and **supermarkets** has a guide to which fish you should and shouldn't be eating. Sadly, most of the tasty ones are off the list, and unless we support the call for **marine reserves** to protect fish stocks and introduce more sustainable fishing practices, the rest may soon follow.

www.mcsuk.org

The Marine Conservation Society works to protect the UK's coasts and seas, and the wildlife that lives in those habitats. Climate change, pollution, the destruction of habitats and the decline of species numbers are all issues with which they are concerned. **What we do** lists their current campaigns, of which **marine reserves** is central. Increasing protected areas in coastal waters will give threatened marine life a chance to re-establish itself, and that can only be of benefit to the complex ocean ecosystems. MSC would like your help with this campaign.

www.oceanalliance.org

Ocean Alliance's boat, the **Odyssey**, recently undertook one of the longest continuous scientific ocean expeditions. She and her crew spent five years collecting data from sperm whales all over the world to help us better understand the spread and severity of pollution in the ocean. **Odyssey video** recorded the voyage on film. **Science in the field** has lots of good stories for teachers and kids. To experience the voyage day by day, click on **Odyssey logs**. The boat is now back and the work of analysing the data has taken over. Watch this space for the results.

OFFICE

....

SEE ALSO: Building Green, Business, Cars, Cleaning Products, Coffee, Computers, Energy, Environment, Packaging, Paper, Reduce-Reuse-Recycle, Waste.

Many of us spend a lot of time at the office. We should make that environment as healthy and sustainable as our homes.

....

www.actionaidrecycling.org.uk

Recycle your ink and toner cartridges, mobile phones and PDAs through ActionAid Recycling, and the proceeds will go to help ActionAid fight world poverty. Close the loop by replacing the empty cartridges with **remanufactured** ones.

www.greenstat.co.uk

The Green Stationery Company specializes in recycled stationery products for the office. Their products are green and competitively priced, with discounts for regular customers. **Why green** will answer your questions as to the benefits of using recycled stationery. They offer Fairtrade freeze-dried **coffee**, and organic tea. You can find compact fluorescent light bulbs and recycling bins under **packaging and facilities products**.

www.green-works.co.uk

Greenworks is a charity that is keeping used office furniture and equipment out of the waste stream by collecting it from donors' offices, and selling it at a low price to new businesses, schools, community groups and others. The collected items are restored, remade or recycled. Click on **donor information** if you have stuff to donate. Greenworks is also active in removing people from the waste stream through their policy of employing and providing certified training for the long-term unemployed. Read about that in **training and employment**, a report in **community information**.

**www.lsx.org.uk/programmes/
greenguide_page1218.aspx**
The London Sustainability Exchange's downloadable **green office guide** has practical advice for small businesses.

www.rabbittrecycling.co.uk
Rabbitt is an acronym of what this company used to do – recycle all bulbs, batteries, inkjets, toners and telephones – but now they handle much more. If your office doesn't recycle everything on their present list, read **UK waste management** and then email them.

www.save-a-cup.co.uk
Encourage your office or workplace to join the Save a Cup Company. They provide a free collection and recycling service to users of hard-walled polystyrene vending cups. **Join Save a Cup** has the registration information. You can buy things made from the recycled cups under **products**. Collect the cups and reduce the waste.

P

PACKAGING

....

www.packaging-technology.com/contractors/containers/eco-pack
Non-toxic packaging that is freezable, microwaveable and biodegradable, and that can be ordered to suit your requirements in the food, medical and automotive industries.

PAPER

....

SEE ALSO: Office, Reduce-Reuse-Recycle, Trees, Waste

Paper manufacturing is the fourth most energy-intensive industry and one of the most polluting. Using recycled paper preserves forests, conserves energy, generates less pollution during manufacturing (because the fibres have already been processed) and reduces solid waste by diverting paper from the waste stream. Recycle all your paper and buy recycled-paper products, including paper towels, toilet paper, gift-wrap, envelopes, greeting cards and stationery. Write to the publishers of your favourite magazines and catalogues and ask them to print their publications on recycled paper.

....

www.evolve-papers.com

One hundred per cent recycled paper that is produced by a closed-loop system. **The evolve solution** explains what that means, and how it works.

www.newscientist.com/news/news.jsp?id=ns99994451

An article in *New Scientist* discusses the ultimate in recycled paper – erasable ink.

www.paperback.coop

Paperback has a wide range of recycled **office** and **graphic** paper. **Presentation** offers a range of custom-made ring-binders, folders and other presentational materials. If you need to persuade the boss to use recycled paper, **myths and facts** has all the arguments.

PEAK OIL

Here's something no one in this oil-dependent, industrial world likes to think about: oil is a finite resource and it will run out. It is getting more expensive to extract, so the price will continue to rise, and that will have a knock-on effect, because we depend on oil for everything: fuel, food, plastics, medicines, industrial production and energy. The question is, what happens when it's gone? Aldous Huxley said, 'Facts do not cease to exist because they are ignored,' and much as we might like to ignore the information on these sites, we would be wiser to acknowledge the facts and start acting on them.

www.lifeaftertheoilcrash.net

Californian lawyer Matt Savinar runs this website, which has been quoted on the floor of the US Congress, in *Fortune* magazine and in the lecture theatres of numerous universities worldwide. It presents many cogent arguments that should persuade everyone to take the issue of peak oil very, very seriously.

www.oilendgame.com

Amory Lovins and his team of writers and researchers from the Rocky Mountain Institute produced this study of how to solve our dependence on oil. It is written for America, but the solutions can be applied in every country in the world. This site offers you the chance to download the book or buy it.

www.powerswitch.org.uk

This site is a wonderful resource for anyone wanting to instigate discussion and raise awareness about the end of the age of oil.

www.wolfatthedoor.org.uk

This website, run by Paul Thomson, an 'ordinary person', presents the complexity of peak oil in terms that other 'ordinary people' can understand.

PEOPLE WHO DID

Paul Thompson is a graphic designer who also designs websites and databases, and for many years environmental issues were just a background noise in his life. He was aware that whales and rainforests needed saving, but didn't really pay much attention. Then on 8 November 2000 he saw an episode of the BBC's *Money Programme* called 'The Last Oil Shock' and discovered the concept of peak oil. However, so far under the public's radar was this concept that when Paul wanted to learn more, he could find very little information on the subject. But in 2003, when he began his own website, he found himself writing about peak oil, and he decided to create a website dedicated to this critical subject. The site now has over forty pages, has been translated into French and now Polish, and has broadened its scope to cover subjects as diverse as alternative energy, agriculture, statistics, permaculture and climate change, all of which are intricately connected to peak oil. Paul has used his graphic skills to design a site that explains this complex issue in simple terms that even a newcomer to the idea of 'peak oil' can understand. His hope is that people will take the information he presents and use it to raise awareness of the issue in their local communities, and that this in turn will start to put pressure on politicians to take the necessary measures to solve this crucial problem before it is too late.

PESTICIDES AND TOXINS

....

SEE ALSO: Batteries, Children, Cleaning Products, Fungi, Garden, Health, Nuclear

....

www.epa.gov/teach/index.html

The US Environmental Protection Agency's searchable database of scientific literature, extending from 1972 to 2003, which contains studies of the effects the environment on the health of children.

www.ewg.org/reports/pfcworld/index.php

Teflon, Goretex, Scotchguard and Stainmaster, brands that we are all familiar with, are products of a chemical group called perfleuorochemicals (PFCs). Recent studies have shown that these are perhaps the most noxious and persistent global contaminants ever made. They are found everywhere: in non-stick cookware, waterproofed clothing, cosmetics, baseball mitts, dental floss, luggage, boots, shoes, gloves, camping equipment, carpets and furniture. The Environmental Working Group has done a detailed analysis of the research, the health hazards, the effects on animals, and the spin connected with PFCs.

www.pan-uk.org

Pesticide Action Network UK is part of an international group working to remove pesticides and other man-made toxins from our world, and to promote the development of safe alternatives to those products. The sustainable farming of healthy foods is a major focus. **Our importance** in **about us** outlines their undertaking. **Community information** has all the resources you need to start clearing pesticides from your home environment. **Pesticide library** takes you to their extensive database. Anyone **concerned about pesticide exposure** should download the leaflet, which offers practical advice as to how to register your concerns, and **publications** is packed with information. **Pesticides in your food** lists the ten foods with the most toxic residues which you should consider replacing with organic alternatives, and while you are on the food page, there are lots of other good links to explore. After all, to quote an old adage, we are what we eat.

www.pesticidedisposal.org
Local council facilities for pesticide disposal.

PLASTIC AND ALTERNATIVES

SEE ALSO: Health, Local Government, Reduce-Reuse-Recycle, Shopping Bags, Waste

The invention of petroleum-based plastics was considered a great benefit to our lives and now they are everywhere: in our toys, cars, computers and game consoles. Our food comes in plastic packaging, we eat off plastic plates with plastic utensils, our water is held in plastic bottles and we drink it from plastic cups, our babies sit in plastic high chairs drinking from plastic bottles. However, it's becoming increasingly clear that petroleum-based plastics are extremely toxic to all life on Earth. A petroleum-based plastic bag can take centuries to decompose in landfill. A biodegradable plastic bag made from corn looks and feels identical, but can decompose in your compost within a month. Biodegradable plastic has been used at several large public gatherings. If you attended the Sydney Olympics in 2000 then you would have eaten food that was served in biodegradable and recyclable containers, and at the end of each day, more than three-quarters of the 660 tons of garbage that had been generated was sent to be composted rather than going to landfill. The production of corn-based plastics uses up to 50 per cent less fossil fuels and emits fewer greenhouse gases than the production of petroleum-based plastics. Many items are now being made with biodegradable plastics based on corn, wheat, peas, potatoes and sugar cane, thus increasing the possibility of the manufacture of plastics becoming part of a closed-loop system. As consumers, we must seek out these products and start rewarding their manufacturers by buying them.

---

www.biobags.co.uk/products.html

Biobags for many uses made from 'GM-free corn starch, vegetable oils and compostable polyesters'. Products also include agricultural-mulch film approved for organic use, compostable cotton buds, golf tees, gloves and aprons, and tableware that can go straight on to the compost heap after the barbecue.

www.biopac.co.uk

Biopac uses renewable plant starch from sugar cane, maize, tapioca and palm leaves to manufacture biodegradable, compostable plastic for use in packaging and displaying foodstuffs, shopping bags and catering. **Environmental** demonstrates the importance of incorporating these kinds of plastics into daily use.

www.firstscience.com/site/articles/sykes.asp
An interesting article about the potential of making biodegradable plastics from bacteria.

www.greengardener.co.uk/pots.htm
Biodegradable garden pots made from coir (coconut fibre).

www.mindfully.org/Plastic/plastic.htm
In-depth information about the harm that petroleum-based plastics may cause to living organisms. Start with **get plastic out of your diet**, and then **plastics: an important part of your healthy diet – think of them as the sixth basic food group**.

safershopping.wwf.org.uk/Range.aspx?id=10
Some glass alternatives to the ubiquitous polycarbonate plastic baby's bottle.

www.wasteonline.org.uk/resources/InformationSheets/Plastics.htm
Waste Online's information sheet on the plastics in your life.

POLLINATORS

SEE ALSO: Biodiversity, Conservation, Gardens

The services of bees, butterflies, birds, bats and moths are absolutely critical for the pollination of 90 per cent of all flowering and domesticated food plants, yet some of our current agricultural and gardening practices are killing them by the billion.

www.beesfordevelopment.org

This group encourages people in poor and remote areas of the world to practise beekeeping, which gives them an income and guarantees the survival of bees. If you are curious about bees, **information centre** might have the answers to your questions.

www.bgci.org/conservation/news/0256

The connection between disappearing bees and disappearing flowers is discussed in this article from Botanic Gardens Conservation International.

www.butterfly-guide.co.uk

This site is full of beautiful photographs and excellent information to help you get to know the butterflies you encounter on nature trails and walks throughout England and Europe. Start with **lifecycle**, which has slideshows of the caterpillar pupating and then hatching into a butterfly. The **UK** page has a **flight time** calendar, and a **site** guide to places where you can visit butterflies.

www.greengardener.co.uk/bee.htm

Help your garden grow by keeping the bees close at hand in beehives designed to attract non-swarming bees.

www.lubee.org/who-whyconserve.aspx

Learn about the critical role that fruit bats play in tropical ecosystems.

www.whatsthiscaterpillar.co.uk

Next time you come across a caterpillar and are curious to know what it will turn into, this site could have the answer. You can add your own photos to the collection, or just browse through the amazing and beautiful ones already there.

Q

QUESTIONS

Good questions are as important as good answers. Here's a question: how can we make environmentally important actions attractive and engaging to the general populace? Please send your answers to: lisa@whatcanidousa.org

R

REDUCE-REUSE-RECYCLE

··

See also: **Batteries, Books, Business, Children, Compost, Computers, Eden Project, Local Government, London, Natural Laws, Office, Shopping Bags, Sustainable Living, Waste, Worms**

Everything you can reuse or recycle is something that doesn't finish up in landfill. Make that a virtue. The Earth's resources are too few and too precious to discard thoughtlessly.

··

www.createuk.com

Create is a community recycling and training charity based in Liverpool that refurbishes donated household appliances and furniture and then sells them at a low price to families in need. By doing this they are providing skilled training and jobs to the unemployed, giving a second life to household goods, and keeping stuff out of landfill. Nothing and nobody is wasted.

www.communityrepaint.org.uk

Here's a way to keep your leftover, reusable house paint out of landfill. Donate it to Community Repaint, and they will distribute it to those who need paint but can't afford it. Click on **where is my nearest scheme** for information. If you want to start such a scheme in your town, then click on **the national network programme**.

www.communitywoodrecycling.org.uk

The National Wood Recycling Project can help you dispose of your waste timber so that it stays out of landfill. **Want to recycle** explains the process.

www.elcrp-recycling.com

'Today the Nightingale Estate - tomorrow the world!' is the motto for the visionary but simple solution that the East London Community Recycling Project came up with to get rid of the rats that plagued the Nightingale Estate in Hackney. All food waste, including meat and fish, is now collected in bins, sprinkled with a mixture of microbes called *bokashi*, collected by ELCRP, put into an oxygen-free composter, and within a fortnight the waste becomes compost. That compost is matured and then given back to the residents of the estate for their gardens and indoor plants. Any leftovers are added to community gardens and green spaces. How simple is that? Your bin is no longer smelly, the problem with rats is gone, and all your food waste is returned to the soil, making it healthier and more productive. This closed-loop system of dealing with food waste sets a great example to local councils and recycling facilities all over the country. Every town and city should have such a system, and when people realize that their food waste is a resource rather than something to put in a plastic bag and throw away, these systems will proliferate. The office of the deputy prime minister and the Scottish Parliament use this system. All other offices throughout the land should click on **consultancy** and follow their example.

www.fareshare.org.uk

FareShare collects excess food from producers and retailers that is usually thrown away, and distributes it to those in need of a good meal throughout the country. **Projects** has contact information for the different regions where FareShare operates, and **what we do** explains how it works.

www.frn.org.uk

Furniture you no longer need doesn't have to clog up landfill. You can donate it to the Furniture Re-use Network, who then refurbish it and make it available to others at a reasonable price. Read Polly Toynbee's article in **social exclusion**, and you will know that you are providing a wonderful service by not throwing that old fridge or table away. Instead, click on **re-use organizations** and find the nearest reuse charity. They will send their free pick-up service to your door.

www.letsrecycle.com/info/localauth/ recycling_officers.jsp

If you have a question about recycling, this site has the contact information for local-authority recycling officers.

www.mercuryrecycling.co.uk

Click on the switch to enter Mercury Recycling Ltd's attractive site. They offer a nationwide mercury-recycling service for all types of lighting and other products that contain mercury, a powerful neurotoxin particularly harmful to young and unborn children. Fish we love to eat – such as tuna, swordfish, mahi mahi and lobster, among many others – are now heavily contaminated with mercury. Mercury Recycling separates the bulbs into their component parts – glass, metal and mercury – all of which are then processed for reuse in new products. This is an example of a closed-loop system at work – nothing is wasted, nothing ends up in landfill. **Why recycle** explains why mercury needs to be kept out of the waste stream. Click on **services** and start recycling your fluorescent bulbs. Households can use the **bulbsafe service** with free pick-up. Everyone is doing it: government offices, hospitals, the railways, prisons, banks, even the Queen. See the list in **clients**, and when you leave the site, don't forget to **switch off**.

www.oxfam.org.uk/what_you_can_do/recycle/index.htm

Oxfam will take your unwanted computers, mobile phones, printer cartridges, foreign currency, stamps, clothes, books, CDs and bric-a-brac, recycle them, and use the money gained to fight poverty.

www.pjprubber.co.uk

PJP recycles car tyres into non-slip, porous, durable rubber slabs that are used for flooring in stables and other animal enclosures. Save on bedding costs, and support a business that keeps tyres out of the waste stream. They also produce mats for children's playgrounds. Click on **colours** to see the decorative inserts available.

www.recycle-more.co.uk

This is your 'one-stop recycling information centre'. **Bank locator** lists your nearest recycling facilities. **Recycling specifics** has the 'what' and 'how' of the recycling process for each category. **Local authorities** can update their information page by clicking on **LA directory**.

www.recyclenow.com

This fresh-looking, easy-to-navigate site is packed with ideas to encourage you to make recycling a habit at home, at school, in the workplace and around town.

www.recycling-guide.org.uk

The words in the left-hand box on the opening page of this colourful, cheerfully informative site say it all. We have to incorporate recycling into our daily lives, and all the resources to do so are here. **Eco-friendly products** under **how to** lists the different eco-friendly symbols that indicate if the product you are buying has been made from recycled materials.

www.reuze.co.uk

The 'how, what, and where to recycle in the UK' site has many ways to recycle stuff, including their free **wanted** and **unwanted** pages, where you can list goods that you want to get rid of, or look for goods that you need.

www.rspb.org.uk/birds/birdwatching/donateoptics/20years.asp

If you have some old binoculars stuffed away in the back of a drawer, donate them to the Royal Society for the Protection of Birds, who will disperse them among the many conservation and education projects they administer in over ninety countries.

www.scrib.org

Never was the subject of steel recycling so colourful. All steel cans are 100 per cent recyclable, and **recycling steel** tells you why you should. The **education zone** has useful material, in both English and Welsh. for teachers to get the message across through writing, science, geography, history, maths and design-technology classes. The sad story of Jak in the film *A Tale of Two Cans*, featured in the interactive quiz, will persuade you never to throw a can away again, ever.

www.sofaproject.org.uk

If you live in the Bath or Bristol area, the Sofa Project will collect your unwanted furniture and appliances, refurbish them and then sell them on at low prices. **Training and volunteers** might have a place for you.

www.thinkcans.com/think_howitworks.asp

Twenty recycled aluminium cans can be made for the same amount of energy that is used to manufacture a new one, so it makes sense to recycle every one you use. You can get cash for them too, and this site tells you how.

www.uk.freecycle.org

Freecycle is a grassroots Internet service that connects anyone in a town wanting to get rid of stuff to anyone in the same town who might want it, at no cost to either. Local volunteers moderate their Freecycle groups. **Joining a group** and **using Freecycle** explain how it works.

PEOPLE WHO DID

The continual stench of rotting food emanating from the huge collecting bins for the tons of domestic rubbish on the Nightingale Estate in Hackney was the final straw for **Cam Matheson**. Cam was the Hackney councillor who had spearheaded the award-winning campaign that removed rubbish, graffiti and flytipping from the local streets, but the problem of household rubbish and the accompanying stink still lingered. As he passed the estate one day and saw rats bustling about among the bins, he decided that composting was the answer. It would remove food from the refuse piles, and the rats would no longer have a source of nourishment, so they too would leave.

Composting was not something that could be easily done on a council estate. The residents would have to be persuaded to separate out their food waste from the rest, and space would have to be found on the estate for compost bins. And how could such a scheme be organized? These problems were no barrier for a Scotsman who had been a mining union organizer. He began seeking ideas from composting organizations. He talked to experts, and as we all do when we become obsessed with a plan, he talked to everyone he met about community composting.

His persistence led him to the Webbs, a family in Cheshire who had invented a composter called the Rocket, which was rat-proof and which could turn food waste into compost in the space of two weeks. Cam knew he had found the answer. He took one back to Hackney and then began an arduous three-year battle to get through the maze of red tape that lay between him and success. During that time he connected with a composting expert, Jane Wilde, and she joined the fight. And when victory was achieved, they then faced the final struggle – how to persuade the residents of the Nightingale Estate to take part in the scheme.

Needless to say, asking most city people if they are interested in composting doesn't result in a resounding 'Yes!' It is so much easier just to throw stuff in the bin. So Cam and Jane reframed their question, and instead asked residents if they wanted to get rid of the rats. There was an instant positive response, and the composting scheme took off. Over seven hundred households joined up, and now fourteen council estates in Hackney are doing it too. One man's simple and sustainable solution for a chronic problem that was blighting his environment, and his patient persistence in seeing that solution through, is an example to us all. It can be done.

S

SCHOOLS

Many of the sites in this book offer school trips.

www.eco-schools.org.uk
Join the eco-schools project and improve your school environment, save money and equip the future generation with the essential skills and values needed to keep the Earth healthy.

www.est.org.uk/schools
Use the Energy Saving Trust's Energy Certification for Schools programme to improve energy-efficiency in your school, and use the money you save to fund other activities.

www.feedmebetter.com
Become part of the community of UK schools that are serving healthy food. Jamie Oliver's site continues the revolution in school dinners.

www.fishandkids.org

A site highlighting the issues of sustainable fishing for children, teachers and the person in charge of school dinners. **Staffroom** has downloadable education packs, activity sheets and slideshows, with a noticeboard for teachers to post comments. **Cafeteria** has suggestions for those responsible for buying food for schools, and **playroom** has a mission for the kids.

www.omlet.co.uk/products_services/ products_services.php?view=Schools

Introduce chickens to the class as a way of teaching them where eggs come from.

organicgardening.org.uk/schools_organic_network

Advice, resources, tools for teachers and an entertaining and informative **noticeboard** are all part of this site, which encourages schools to learn how to grow an organic garden.

www.walktoschool.org.uk

Schools all over Britain are joining the walk-to-school campaign, which encourages children to be healthier and more self-confident, and aims to keep traffic jams around school gates to a minimum. There are resources for **schools, parents, pupils** and **local authorities** to promote the programme. The **WoW!** scheme rewards schools and participating pupils for consistently walking to school one day each week. Click on the **school e-pals** button and share your experiences with others who are also walking to school.

SHOPPING BAGS

Single-use, plastic shopping bags are made from oil. Though handy, their manufacture is a waste of a precious resource and their disposal causes big problems. We have become used to the plastic shopping bags that shopkeepers and supermarkets give us – we use ten billion every year, but when we throw them away they lie in landfill sites indefinitely, where they can take five hundred or more years to decompose, slowly leaching their toxins into the soil and water. If left to blow in the wind they can become deadly food for seabirds, sea turtles and whales, or accumulate as tiny, long-lived fragments in the ocean – a serious and growing hazard to marine life, and yet another way for their toxins to enter our food. When a marine animal that has eaten a plastic bag dies, it decays, but the bag survives to be eaten by and so kill another animal. Towns all over the world are successfully declaring themselves plastic-bag free. Taiwan began to systematically ban them in 2001. Bangladesh banned them outright in 2002. Aberdeen is instigating a 'Fantastic it's not plastic!' campaign and giving cloth shopping bags away free to shoppers on a trial basis. Start eradicating plastic shopping bags from your life by taking reusable bags with you every time you shop. Keep some in the car for that unexpected impulse buy. Get creative, make some, and give them away for Christmas presents.

www.canby.co.uk
Biodegradable jute shopping bags made by a carbon-neutral company, which can be produced with printed logos.

www.plasticshoppingbagfree.org.nz

This group of women in Golden Bay in New Zealand, inspired by a similar group in Coles Bay in Australia, decided that there would be no more plastic bags in their town, and they succeeded in eliminating them. **Global news** has stories of what other countries are doing about the problem, and **facts and figures** explains why plastic bags are such a bad idea.

www.reusablebags.com/news.php?id=12

This page from Reusable Bags will keep you abreast of the news about plastic-bag use in Britain.

SIMPLE STEPS

Simple things anyone can do:

➲ Don't leave the tap running when shaving, brushing teeth or hand-washing dishes.

➲ Turn off lights you're not using.

➲ Turn off computers and monitors when you leave them for more than an hour.

➲ Unplug electrical chargers when not in use.

➲ Don't leave the TV or stereo system on standby.

➲ Replace your most-used incandescent bulbs with compact fluorescents.

➲ Look for the Energy Efficiency logo when buying new appliances.

➲ Choose some or all of your food from organic and local sources.

➲ Don't fill the kettle to boil water for one cup of tea.

- ⮌ Don't put hot food in the fridge, or leave its door open longer than necessary.
- ⮌ Walk, cycle, go by bus or car-share instead of driving.
- ⮌ Use pump sprays, not aerosols.
- ⮌ Always have shopping bags and a bag for rubbish in your car.
- ⮌ Use cloth napkins instead of paper ones.
- ⮌ Buy in bulk to reduce packaging waste.
- ⮌ Use a clothes line rather than a tumble dryer whenever possible.
- ⮌ Recycle.
- ⮌ Compost.
- ⮌ Think before you buy.

SMOKING

Smoking is a personal choice, but one that is becoming increasingly unpopular, thanks to the documented effects of cigarettes on air pollution and second-hand smoke on non-smokers, not to mention the now solidly proven health problems associated with smoking itself.

www.ash.org.uk

'One in two long-term smokers will die prematurely as a result of smoking – half of these in middle age.' *ASH Fact Sheet 2.*

Action on Smoking and Health is committed to saving the lives of those 114,000 people in the UK who die each year from the effects of this activity, and making sure that others do not sacrifice themselves on the altar of tobacco companies' profits. **Facts, stats and pics** tells you the real story. **Quitting tips and help** has ASH's **fifteen top tips to stopping smoking** and many other resources offering support.

www.bhf.org.uk/smoking

The opening image of this British Heart Foundation site says it all. Joining a support group is a proven way to stop smoking. Find the nearest one here.

SURFING

www.sas.org.uk

Click on **the problem**, read the contents, and you will know why in 1990 a group of 'aquatic eco-warriors' joined forces to fight for a pollution-free ocean. Their targets include the three hundred million gallons of raw or partially treated sewage that is spewed daily into the UK's coastal waters, and the huge amounts of toxic waste that end up in the oceans. One of their **solutions** is for water to be reclaimed from properly treated sewage and reused to clean cars, water crops and golf courses, in cooling industrial processes and to maintain wetlands. Surfers Against Sewage's **research** is now helping to develop government policies on water health, and in the **future**, with their focus extending to climate change and alternative energies, the impact of their voice will grow stronger.

SUSTAINABLE LIVING

SEE ALSO: **every other entry in this book**

'Sustainability means that as a society we are aware of the impact of our actions on the planet, that we take responsibility for these actions and are transparent in our processes. It requires that we have a vision for our future, educate ourselves to decrease our negative impact on the earth whilst seeking ways to reduce damage to the planet.' Sustainable Living Foundation Forum, Melbourne, April 2000.

Living sustainably means living so that our present needs are met without compromising the needs of future generations.

www.beyondgreen.co.uk

Beyond Green is a group of sustainability experts – scientists, architects, urban planners, ecologists, communicators – who 'conceive, plan, design, communicate, consult on, train, develop business models for and help to deliver sustainable developments.' They are at the centre of many of Britain's urban-regeneration projects. One of the directors is Joanne Yarrow, who is perhaps better known as the 'green expert' on ITV1's *This Morning*. Click on **what we do – projects by category–housing** and download *Six Steps*, a report done for the Housing Corporation on sustainable housing associations.

www.bioregional.com

It is said that the eco-footprint of the average UK resident is such that if everyone else in the world had a similar lifestyle, there would have to be two more planets to sustain us all. BioRegional is working to help us change the size of our eco-footprint in many areas – housing, paper production, wood products, food, transport and textiles – without drastically cutting back on our quality of life. **Eco-footprinting** in **about us** explains the issue. **Projects** introduces their five main programmes, with links to many connected projects, e.g. restoring the old **local lavender** beds of south London; **BedZED**, the award-winning eco-village development; the triumphant story of the making of a **bio-fuel sports car**; and recycling your business paper and cardboard with **the laundry**. The House of Commons participates in BioRegional's **local paper for London** scheme, which means they recycle paper, then buy locally produced recycled paper, thus closing the loop – what was waste is reused. This site is full of exciting ideas and solutions for how we can **take action** to live more lightly and therefore more happily on the Earth.

www.cat.org.uk

The Centre for Alternative Technology began in 1973 as a small group of people interested in pursuing a way of life that was in accordance with natural laws, rather than one that followed the mainstream path based on industrial and economic growth. Now the centre has become a 'showcase for sustainable development', with a salaried staff of over a hundred, many more enthusiastic volunteers and an annual turnover in the millions. **Visit CAT** introduces the visitor centre, which you get to by means of a water-powered cliff railway. Open seven days a week, the centre offers an education in how to live more lightly on the Earth. You can see solar-, biomass-, wind-, hydro- and wave-energy generation at work, compost growing and composting toilets, and a collection of environmentally responsible buildings. There are gardens, animals, interactive exhibitions, playgrounds and a Mole Hole, which the children will love. **Virtual tour** has the layout. There's a free **information** service to answer all your questions about how to reduce the impact of your ecological footprint. **Education** offers a downloadable *Where's the Impact* teaching resource. **Greenshop** is crammed with ideas to support your green way of life. **Membership** has many benefits, and **consultancy** offers consumers the expertise from over thirty years of seeking alternative technologies to those that have been so damaging to the Earth.

www.environ.org.uk/ecohouse/index.php

If you want to see how an environmentally friendly house functions, visit Leicester's famous EcoHouse. There are interactive displays, tons of ideas and information, an **organic garden**, **café** and **shop** where they sell green products, and there is help for those interested in applying for grants to assist with their own eco-home improvements.

The **EcoHouse training room** is available for hire. They also offer **guided tours**, and welcome **school visits**. Anyone interested in helping out should click on **volunteering**.

www.grownupgreen.org.uk

If you've ever quailed at the thought of how difficult it would be to live in a more sustainable way, then this site will take you by the hand and gently but firmly set you on that path. Their stated aim is to educate the public about the importance of protecting and improving the world in which we live, and **library** is a good place to start. By becoming a member you can submit articles or write about your personal eco-experiences, and **news** will keep you up to date.

www.harlownorth.com/environmental_sustainability.php

The new town of Harlow North is being designed to be 'an exemplary environmentally sustainable development'. Find out what that means on this site. Comments and questions are welcomed in **have your say**.

www.hockertonhousingproject.org.uk

The Hockerton Housing Project in Nottinghamshire is an award-winning example of a sustainable community. Take the **virtual tour**, then if you are interested in seeing the real thing, or joining in a workshop or masterclass, **HHP events and tours** has the information to enable you to do that. **Additional services** includes the free **eco matchmaking service**, to connect those looking for others interested in building sustainable communities like the one at Hockerton.

www.leicesterbetterbuildings.org.uk

The benefits of sustainable building are well expressed in this site, which celebrates and explains the decisions that led to Leicester being declared the UK's first 'Environment City'. There is information here for everyone involved in the urban-regeneration process, and for those who will live and work in the developments being built to these new environmental standards, which encompass energy and water use, waste disposal, land use, transport, and the well-being and health of those using the buildings. **Key topics** has information on all these issues, including **building materials**; there is a list of **case studies** showing what can be done. **Whole life costs**, which can be found in **principles**, lays out one of the fundamental reasons why sustainable living needs to be central to the way we all live from now on.

www.primrosetrust.org.uk

The Primrose Trust is an educational centre for sustainable living in the village of Felindre, in Powys, Wales. Its focus is on education, with progammes for schools on how to look after the Earth and why that is necessary, the connection between people, plants and their shared environment, and how the quality of our lives improves when we grow our own food. Some of the classes are taught in the new Celtic roundhouse that was built by volunteers from many countries. There are also **courses** for gardeners, farmers, smallholders and retirees – in fact, anyone wanting to learn the skills of permaculture.

T

TEACHERS

Educators are on the frontline of the battle to engage and excite young minds about the overwhelming complexity of the environmental problems we face. Here is some ammunition for that fight.

earthballoon.com/resource.htm
An extensive list of links for teaching about the environment.

www.farmtrails.org.uk/index.html
Take the class for a walk round an organic farm, not all of which are in the middle of the countryside. The **teachers** page has all the links you will need to make it an unforgettable trip.

www.froglife.org/workingwithsecondaryschools.htm
Resource material about amphibians and reptiles for secondary-school teachers.

www.hockertonhousingproject.org.uk
'The educational opportunities available at Hockerton are arguably without parallel in the country and Nottinghamshire schools are very lucky to have this provision on their doorstep. It would be great to see many more schools taking pupils to your site . . .'

Environmental Education, Nottinghamshire County Council, November 2005.

This award-winning community offers students of all ages a chance to see what is meant by a sustainable way of life. **Education services** lays out the programmes they offer to all levels – primary, secondary, college and university.

www.journeytoforever.org

Journey to Forever is an overland expedition from Hong Kong, through Asia and Africa, to Cape Town, a distance of 25,000 miles. As the participants travel through remote areas of the world, they work with local NGOs on rural-development projects and connect to the world through the Internet to report on the sustainable farming practices and technologies they see being used. There are many resources for schools on this site. Children from all over the world can connect with each other to discover what is being done in other countries and cultures to help keep the planet healthy. **Internet** links you to a long list of servers, each with their own specialities. Young poets can post their work on this site. The links are comprehensive – a journey in themselves.

www.littlerotters.org.uk

Little Rotters is a programme created by schools to teach composting in schools. Little Rotters clubs are run by children, in the hope that they will take what they learn about the wonders of compost back home, and encourage the return of organic waste to the soil rather than adding it to landfill. The soil needs it more. Click on **free handbook** and get the *Little Rotters Composting Handbook* delivered free to your primary school, start a club, and reduce the amount of compostable waste thrown away by the school.

www.pathfinderscience.net
Great ideas for science projects.

www.pbs.org/odyssey/class/index.html
Use the whales in **class from the sea** to get children interested in the oceans.

www.rmi.org/sitepages/pid468.php
Rocky Mountain Institute for Kids offers excellent classroom-resource materials on energy and water.

THERMOSTATS

You can cut your carbon-dioxide emissions by over 5 per cent and save an average of thirty pounds a year if you turn the thermostat down by just one degree Celsius.

TOURISM

SEE ALSO: Bicycles, Cars, Golf, Volunteering

Tourism can have a big effect on the places and people you visit. More and more people are becoming interested in eco-tourism – a way of travelling that protects the environment, improves the well-being of local people, and makes them stakeholders in maintaining their ecosystems.

www.ecotourism.org
The International Ecotourism Society offers resources for travellers and for those in the travel business.

www.ecotours.co.nz
The attractions of New Zealand's fragile and special land have created a tourist industry that is central to that country's economy. But care must be taken to preserve the ecosystems of the unique fauna and flora that inhabit these remote islands. Eco-tours encourages operators to practise sustainable tourism, believing that this is one of the best ways to secure the future of New Zealand's unique beauty. Print out the **travel map** to see what's on offer, and then click on **guides** to find out where you want to go. **Top ten guides** leads you to the best trips.

www.evrental.com
Rent a hybrid car from America's first environmentally friendly car-rental company.

www.green-business.co.uk
Any traveller concerned about their environmental impact should look at the destinations and accommodation listed on this site. Green Tourism Business Scheme runs an accreditation service for best environmental practice in the tourism industry. **Case studies** shows how environmental care can also save money. If you want to register your business, start at **green health check**.

www.greenchoices.com/id42.htm
Green Choices offers eco-travel opportunities in Africa, Canada, South and Central America, plus a world guide to volunteering for nature-conservation programmes.

www.greenhotels.com

Green Hotels aim to reduce solid waste and save water and energy. Members receive *Guidelines and Ideas* – 110 pages of environmentally friendly ways to save money while saving the Earth. Travellers can find addresses on the site for green hotels throughout the USA, Canada, South America, the Caribbean, Europe and Africa, as well as green travel hints that include what to do before you leave home.

www.orangutan.org.uk

The Orangutan Foundation offers **tours** for visitors to see these enchanting but endangered primates in Borneo's rainforest.

www.organicholidays.com

A list of farms, bed and breakfasts, guesthouses and small hotels worldwide that offer accommodation accompanied by the pleasures of organic produce.

www.responsibletravel.com

This site puts you in contact with over 170 leading tourism businesses from around the world that offer a wide choice of eco-friendly holidays, ranging from a farm in New Zealand to volunteering to study climate change in the Arctic.

www.waterscape.com

Use the British Waterways site to plan a holiday exploring the **waterways** of Britain. The **wildlife guide** introduces the many friends you might see on your way. Click on **go fishing** to buy a **licence**, locate your **local fishery**, and use the **species guide** to determine what you've caught.

http://h.webring.com/hub?ring=ecotouring
There is somewhere for everyone in this extensive list of
eco-tourism sites from all over the world.

TOURISM: CRUISE SHIPS

*Despite the glossy brochures advertising the pleasures
of cruise ships, they are major ocean polluters. Both of
the following groups are working to remedy that
situation.*

www.bluewaternetwork.org/campaign_ss_cruises.shtml

www.oceana.org/index.php?id=91

www.freighterworld.com
An alternative to a luxury cruise, which is very damaging
to the oceans, would be to take a trip on a freighter. This
site offers comfortable, relaxing, informal ocean travel
without the crowds.

TOURISM: ECO-RESORTS

*Eco-resorts are becoming destinations of choice for many
travellers who are concerned about the environmental impact
of their holidays. These resorts are built and run according
to strict sustainable practices, with minimal land-clearing,
renewable energy, solar-heated water, compostable toilets
and grey-water systems. The energy-efficient buildings are*

made from sustainable and non-toxic materials. Food is grown locally and food waste is composted. Conservation and support of the local community are an integral part of an eco-resort. Here are a few of the most beautiful I have found, which I would love to see one day.

www.bayoffires.com.au

Two ecological adventures in Tasmania. Choose either a six-day walk through serene mountains, still lakes and deep forests, or a four-day trek along the Bay of Fires on the edge of Mount William National Park.

www.polepole.com

Pole Pole is a resort in the Mafia Island Marine Park, a protected ecosystem in Tanzania. The magazine *Travel and Leisure* has named it one of the world's best eco-lodges.

www.shompole.com

This luxury safari camp in Kenya at the edge of the Great Rift Valley is run in partnership with the local Masai people. Funds from this camp go towards schools, clinics and the maintenance of the prolific wildlife in the surrounding area.

www.tiamoresorts.com/world.html

Billed as the 'Caribbean's most environmentally sensitive hotel operation', this award-winning Bahamian resort is working hard to set new standards in eco-sensitive resort development.

TRANSPORTATION

See also: Action, Architecture, Bicycles, Business, Cars, Climate Change, Design, Films, Global Warming, Hydrogen Fuel Cells, London, Peak Oil, Schools, Walking

Although most of us find the ease of using a car irresistible, that mode of transport is also very costly to the planet. Here are some alternative ways of getting from A to B.

www.eta.co.uk

The Environmental Transport Association is the first motoring organization in the world to offset its carbon emissions and become carbon neutral. Based in Weybridge, it is an ethical insurance company that will insure houses, travel, bicycles and vehicles. But its mission is to encourage the public to use the car less, and alternative means of transport more. **Green issues** puts their case. There's a **car buyer's guide** to help those seeking greener vehicles, and information about the annual **in-town-without-my-car day** celebrated throughout Europe in September.

www.mobilityweek-europe.org

Each September since 2000, many UK cities have joined others in Europe to celebrate European Mobility Week. Events highlight sustainable mobility – walking, cycling, public transport – and culminate in a **car-free day**. Each week has a **theme**, and **participating cities** are listed, with activities. If yours isn't on the list, click on **how to participate** and start to get your city involved. **Responsible car use** has some good ideas for activities.

www.powabyke.com

Electric bikes and scooters can get you around town efficiently. Click on **salary sacrifice** and get a half-price bike with the help of the boss.

www.scootelectric.co.uk

Click on **the big picture** and see why getting an electric scooter might be a good idea.

www.seat61.com

The Man in Seat Sixty-One, Mark Smith, who has inside knowledge of how railways work, has developed this site to make rail travel easier for those who would prefer to go by train rather than plane. Everything you need to know about rail travel worldwide is here. **What's new** has updated information, and **about me** has the story. **Useful links** connects you to a currency converter, passport and visa information, tourist offices, foreign-office advice and many other essential elements for trouble-free travel.

www.sustrans.org.uk

'Be admired for the car you don't drive' is the motto of Sustrans, a charity that wants us to get on our bikes, our feet, on buses and trains – anything, as long as we are not in our cars. They want us all to get about in a way that is healthier for us and the rest of life on Earth. They are building the National Cycle Network that passes within a mile of half the population. **Get cycling** has maps of bike trails all over the UK, and information for those interested in **commuting by bike**. Other **projects** include the creation of **safe routes to schools** and **liveable neighbourhoods**. Artists might be able to become involved with the **art and the travelling landscape** project.

www.transport2000.org.uk

An independent national group that promotes sustainable transport systems that can reduce car use nationally, through lobbying and campaigning, and locally, by working with communities to help them develop green travel plans. **Change your streets** has a toolkit for local campaigners wanting to slow down drivers. **Platform network** is pressing for better rail services, especially in rural areas, and to get freight off the roads and on to the railways.

www.vectrix.co.uk

Take a look at the world's first high-performance electric scooter, which has a top speed of sixty-two mph, rapid acceleration, and batteries capable of taking it seventy miles on a single charge. It's a thing of beauty that can remove vehicle pollution and trips to petrol stations from your life.

TREES

SEE ALSO: Action, Architecture, Biodiversity, Building Green, Business, Climate Change, Community, Conservation, Endangered Species, Environment, Gardens, National Parks, Natural Laws, Volunteering, Reduce-Reuse-Recycle, Waste

Trees evolved about forty million years ago, long before dinosaurs walked the Earth, and they have been essential to the well-being of life on Earth ever since. They provide a habitat for countless species. They keep water healthy and prevent erosion. By absorbing carbon dioxide and producing oxygen, they keep our air fresh, and these days this process is essential for slowing the effects of global warming – to counteract the greenhouse emissions of cars, every driver should plant at least seven trees every year.

However, the pressure of human needs is beginning to threaten forests all over the world.

....

www.forests.org
The Forest Conservation Portal is a gateway to over three thousand sites addressing forest ecology issues, deforestation and its consequences, the vital importance of the rainforest, and the absolute necessity to harvest all forests sustainably.

www.native-tree-shop.com
The Woodland Trust, in conjunction with Alba Trees, runs this website, offering a range of native trees and shrubs that are delivered to your door ready to be planted. Instructions for planting are on the website.

www.the-tree.org.uk
This is a beautiful, imaginative and informative site. Mythology, facts, botany, spiritual connections, photographs, proverbs, articles, environmental issues, the art of pruning, agroforestry and reforestation, traditions and philosophy, creation myths and an art gallery all take their part in celebrating the central role that trees play in our lives. **Ancient yews** in **action-environment** has wonderful information about the mythology surrounding these ancient trees, and the campaign to document and save these monuments to life.

www.treecouncil.org.uk
The Tree Council loves trees, and is doing everything it can to encourage us to do the same. The programme has many initiatives: the annual Walk in the Woods, Seed-Gathering Sunday and Trees Love Care, to help people look after trees they have planted. There are **tree grants**

available for communities and schools, to encourage the planting of even more trees, and if you love trees, you might be interested in becoming a **tree warden** in your local community.

www.treesforcities.org

This charity plants trees all around the town, in many cities round the world, to restore beauty and wildlife habitats, as well as to counteract the effects of global warming. They encourage the involvement of young people in their planting programmes, but welcome volunteers of all ages. Their annual tree-athalon (www.tree-athalon.org) raises money that will enable them to plant thousands of trees in cities from London to Peru. **City projects** lists where the trees are being planted, and **information and reports** has **tree facts**, **trees and carbon**, and descriptions of **native trees** to help you decide which variety you might like to donate to the growing urban forests.

www.woodland-trust.org.uk

For over thirty years, the Woodland Trust has been saving threatened ancient woodland and creating new areas of native woodland throughout the UK. This well-designed site is packed with information. Scroll through their **family of websites** and discover how **legacies** can help to restore ancient woodlands and create new ones; help augment the map of ancient trees by joining the **ancient tree hunt**; record your own nature diary on **enaturenotes**; if you live near Hull, check out **Hull tree for all**, and join the action. Recycle your old mobile phone and help plant more trees by clicking on **shops** then **greener lifestyle**. Buy trees and other imaginative gifts that will help the Earth in the **shop**.

U

UNIVERSE

See the glory of the Universe, within which our Earth is but a speck.

antwrp.gsfc.nasa.gov/apod
Each day receive a different, stunning image of the universe, along with a professional astronomer's explanation of what you're seeing.

www.britastro.org/dark-skies/index.html
Light pollution prevents us from seeing the stars, and the Campaign for Dark Skies wants to change that. If we can illuminate our nights with outdoor lights that only shine downwards, then we can reclaim the heavens. **The issues** sheds further light.

www.nineplanets.org
Take a multi-media tour of the solar system and study current scientific knowledge in conjunction with the mythology about our neighbouring planets and their moons.

V

VINEGAR

SEE ALSO: Cleaning Products, Health, Pesticides and Toxins

You can use white-wine vinegar as a cleaner, to help with the laundry and to get bugs off plants. If I have burnt a saucepan, I soak it overnight with vinegar and a little water, and the next morning it is easy to clean. Use the following sites to find out more about this inexpensive, non-toxic cleaner.

www.superbherbs.net/sec6.htm
More ways to use vinegar, including removing chewing gum from the carpet and cleaning the leather sofa.

www.thenewhomemaker.com/node/277
The New Homemaker's list of the many ways you can use vinegar.

www.versatilevinegar.org
The Vinegar Institute says, 'One bottle of white distilled vinegar contains a whole shelf's worth of specialized cleaners'. Here you will find the history of this ten-thousand-year-old product that has been made commercially since 2000 BC. Click on **uses and tips** and see what it can do for you.

VOLUNTEERING

....

All over the world, environmental organizations depend on the willing spirit of those who are happy to give their time and energy to help save our planet in return for the experience of a lifetime, a great gap year, the chance to find out what you want to do with the rest of your life, or all of the above. For those who want to stay closer to home, nearly every site in this book has opportunities for volunteers.

....

www.bdmlr.org.uk/pages/main.html

British Divers Marine Life Rescue began in 1988 when a group of divers joined the rescue effort for some dying harbour seals in the Wash. Now it provides a twenty-four-hour marine animal rescue service throughout the UK. Their teams are all trained volunteers, and you don't need to be a diver to join up – **training** will tell you more. **Rescue** has lists of strandings that BDMLR have assisted with, and the **help page** has the information you'll need to identify a beached animal.

www2.btcv.org.uk

British Trust for Conservation Volunteers runs a nationwide volunteering programme for cleaning up and restoring local environments. Join **green gyms** and exercise three hours a week, while working in the open air. **Network** links you to **breathing spaces**, a joint venture with the BBC to help neighbourhoods create the green spaces that people and wildlife need. There are training progammes where you can **learn** practical skills that will be useful for life or a career, and lots of activities for those **under twenty-five** in **volunteer**.

www.conservationvolunteers.org/members.htm

The Conservation Volunteer Alliance has members in many countries, and this page will link to them.

www.crossculturalsolutions.org

Cross-Cultural Solutions takes volunteers to Latin America, Asia, Russia and Africa, and works to build understanding and peace. CNN called this 'an amazingly humane and caring organization'.

www.csv.org.uk

Community Services Volunteers connects those interested in volunteering to projects that need them. **Volunteer** has information for people of all ages.

www.ecovolunteer.org

Work with Przewalski's horses in Mongolia, wolves and Karakachan shepherd dogs in the mountains of Bulgaria, watch belugas mating and giving birth during the white nights near the Solovetski Islands in Russia, or help in a new study to find out how orangutans self-medicate in Northern Sumatra. These are a few of the many exciting choices offered to you by Ecovolunteer.

www.greenvol.com

Green Volunteers – a worldwide guide to voluntary work in nature conservation.

www.gvi.co.uk

Global Vision International uses volunteers from all over the world to work on aid-related projects. Enjoy a wildlife-conservation expedition to the Amazon rainforest, take part in a marine-life census in the Seychelles, or become part of the South African National Parks Internship Programme. Minimum age is eighteen.

www.wwoofinternational.org/home

Willing Workers on Organic Farms is an international programme that connects students and other travellers with organic farms throughout the world. The host family provides food and accommodation in exchange for four to six hours' work a day. The WWOOFERS experience organic farming, develop skills in self-sufficiency and learn about the area they are visiting, and both parties have a chance to learn about each other's culture.

WALKING

SEE ALSO: Cars, Hiking, Keep UK Beautiful, London, National Parks, Schools

Walking is healthy, causes no pollution and is a free mode of transport.

www.livingstreets.org.uk/about.htm

Reclaim your streets from the roar of traffic with the help of Living Streets. This nationwide campaign run by the Pedestrian Association is not anti-car, it's just pro-people being able to stroll safely in their streets. Scroll down through **about us** and read the **ten liveability criteria**. They will help you decide whether you and your neighbours need to join the campaign and reclaim your local streets. There are also **consultancy services** to help those in the business of town-planning give priority to pleasant walking spaces within communities.

www.peaktopeak.net

A worldwide compendium of walking and backpacking sites. Use the links to hiking clubs worldwide to find a local walking companion.

www.ramblers.org.uk
For over seventy years, the Ramblers' Association has been championing the benefits of walking for all comers. **Get walking** will get you started, if you haven't already. Once you are on the path, **our work** lists the issues you might get involved with to keep those paths clear. **Discover your region** links you to walks in your area.

www.waterscape.com/walking
Stroll along one of the many canals and rivers threading their peaceful way through town and country.

WASTE

SEE ALSO: Architecture, Batteries, Building Green, Business, Compost, Conscious Consumerism, Eden Project, Farming, Home, Junk Mail, Keep UK Beautiful, Local Government, Mobile Phones, Nappies, Natural Laws, Oceans, Office, Pesticides and Toxins, Plastic and Alternatives, Reduce-Reuse-Recycle, Schools, Shopping Bags, Sustainable Living, Tourism, Worms

'Zero Waste is an extraordinary concept that can lead society, business and cities to innovative breakthroughs that can save the environment, lives and money.' Paul Hawken.

Waste is one of our major problems. Today's delight becomes tomorrow's rubbish, and the Earth is dying under the pressure. It is becoming more and more difficult to cope with the amount of waste we produce. Many of the things we dump are full of toxic substances that filter into the soil and groundwater, eventually entering the food chain and from there our bodies. The natural world really

*has no such thing as true waste, because one species'
waste is another's resource. Like it or not, human beings
are part of the natural world, and therefore must obey
natural laws – laws that are far more powerful than any
that governments can pass. So we too must turn all our
waste into resources, which is what the Zero Waste
movement is all about. By recognizing that waste is a
resource in disguise, and using nature's closed-loop
system as its model, this movement is building a new
industrial revolution for the twenty-first century.*

------

www.loopsolutions.co.uk
Loop is a recycling company offering a closed-loop waste
service for businesses and the public sector.

www.matta-products.com
Matta Products (UK) Ltd recycles waste plasticized
rubber and PVC into recyclable surfacing material that
can be used for safety in playgrounds, industrial areas
and swimming pools, as well as land retention – another
example of waste being reused, instead of just filling the
landfill.

www.wastebook.org
Waste Watch magazine called this 'one of, if not the most,
comprehensive regional waste guides available on the
Net'.

www.wasteonline.org.uk
This excellent site is the information branch of
the environmental charity Waste Watch
(www.wastewatch.org.uk). Before you do anything else,
click on **wacky waste facts** and learn how big a problem
waste is for us all. **Waste at home** has great information

for householders; **subject A–Z** introduces what you can do with an extensive list of things such as CDs and coat-hangers, water-filters and medicines; and there are **information sheets** to answer all your questions. Use this site to help you start reusing the waste in your life.

www.zwia.org
The Zero Waste International Alliance is aiming for 'a world without waste', which means removing landfill and incinerators from our lives and using what was in them as a resource for economic opportunity. **Publications** in **news** lists communities worldwide who have started on a zero-waste path, including some in the UK. **Standards** lays out the goals for any business or community wanting to adopt Zero Waste.

WASTES, HAZARDOUS

www.chem-away.org.uk
Enter your postcode and find out where you can safely dispose of garden chemicals.

www.oilbankline.org.uk
Engine oil is a serious pollutant. It must be disposed of responsibly, and this site will help you find the most convenient place to do that.

WATER

SEE ALSO: **Action, Architecture, Building Green, Composting Toilets, Eden Project, Environment, Gardens, Green Roofs, Home, Local Government, Sustainable Living**

'About one third of the world's population already lives in countries considered to be "water stressed" - that is, where consumption exceeds 10 per cent of total supply. If present trends continue, two out of every three people on Earth will live in that condition by 2025.' Kofi Annan, We The Peoples, 2000

Less than 1 per cent of the Earth's water is fresh water suitable for domestic use, irrigation and industry. By 2025, the UN expects that 3.5 billion people will experience water shortages, as aquifers dry up, rivers dwindle and droughts spread. In August 2006, the WWF warned that rich countries would have to drastically rethink the way they handle water if they want to avoid the impending water crisis that is already plaguing poorer nations. Water conservation is one of the first steps in sustainable living. Pollution of freshwater from storm-water run-off and agricultural and industrial practices is also a serious problem. Nothing can live without fresh, clean water.

www.clear-water-revival.com

This beautiful site, with its peaceful sounds of life by a country pond, introduces a company that creates **natural swimming pools**, ponds and lakes. They also construct **reed-bed** water-treatment systems, which are the natural way to dispose of agricultural waste and nutrient run-off, household waste-water and storm-water run-off.

www.earthday.net

Click on **programs and campaigns** and then **water for life** and download fact sheets to learn about how communities around the world find solutions to their water problems. Click on **ten thirsty children** to learn about the challenges faced by young children worldwide as they struggle to find fresh water.

www.elementalsolutions.co.uk

This company specializes in ecological waste-water treatment, utilizing waterless urinals, composting toilets, reed beds and sewage systems where there are no mains connections.

www.freerain.co.uk

Rainwater management systems for **domestic** and **commercial** properties.

www.greenbuildingstore.co.uk/water.php

Water-saving devices from the Green Building Store.

www.greywaterirrigation.co.uk

Save water by installing a grey-water system that uses the waste-water from your sink, shower, washing machine and bath to water the garden, and even in a drought your plants will thrive.

www.livingmachines.com

Living Machines Inc. builds solar-powered waste-water systems that mimic Nature by using micro-organisms, plants, fish and small invertebrates to process sewage and waste-water. The end product is recyclable water that can be used to water parks, gardens and golf courses; help with cooling industrial plants; flush toilets; and aid in construction work, fire-fighting and washing your car. This is another good example of the closed-loop system. The Living Machine system at Ethel M Chocolates, in Las Vegas, Nevada (www.ethelm.com) – click on **the living machine** at the bottom of the page – treats thirty-two thousand gallons of highly concentrated industrial waste-water a day, and reuses it to irrigate their famous cactus garden. At present the biggest of these systems is in Wyong, Australia, where Master Foods processes the two hundred thousand gallons of waste-water used in its food-production process per day. Click on **living machine systems** to see the variety of businesses worldwide that have installed these natural systems to handle their waste-water.

www.newint.org/issue354/facts.htm

This in-depth look at the facts underlying the global water crisis has graphs, charts, pictures and articles about potential wars over water, harvesting raindrops, and the availability of water and who owns it.

www.ozh2o.com

Water facts abound in this Australian site that celebrates Planet Water.

www.rainharvesting.co.uk

Harvest the rain, and save it for a dry day. Rainharvesting Systems has been in the business since 1994 and offers a wide range of equipment and expertise. Stored rainwater can be used to flush toilets, do the laundry and water the garden, thus helping to conserve precious drinking water. **Water conservation** explains why we should. **Design** will help you **calculate** what size tank you may need and how much water you could save, and there is a **simple**

quotation form to fill out. **Systems** introduces what's on offer, whether it's for domestic purposes, or for something bigger like a school or industrial premises.

www.ukrivers.net/index.html
The UK Rivers network is working for the healthy future of rivers. This site is an excellent resource for those interested in how pollution affects our waters, and how to clean them up.

www.waterstewards.org
The Water Stewards Network has arisen as a result of the global movement to privatize water and the information on this site questions this trend. **Water crisis** spells out the problem, and under **privatization** there is an excellent video from Public Citizen that expresses the issue clearly. **Sustainable technologies** has some suggestions for handling water at a local level.

www.waterwise.org.uk
On this site you will find **water-saving tips** and **efficiency devices** to help stem the flow.

WEDDINGS

SEE ALSO: Gifts, Tourism

www.eco-wedding.com
Use this site to help you plan a green wedding.

WORMS

....

SEE ALSO: Compost, Gardens

Remove your food waste from the rubbish bin and put your own worm farm to work converting it into nutrient-rich, 100 per cent organic fertilizer for the potted plants and garden. This is something schools and businesses could utilize as well.

....

www.alphawaves.net/meadow
If you live in Scotland you could buy your worms from Dumfriesshire.

www.greengardener.co.uk/worms.htm
Buy your worm farm here, feed the worms all the fruit and vegetable scraps from the kitchen, and they'll give you back excellent compost and a concentrated liquid fertilizer. That's a closed-loop system at work.

www.vermitech.com/worm_fr.htm
How worms work – the biology of earthworms.

www.wormsdirectuk.co.uk
Worms for composting, pet food and fishing.

X

X CHROMOSOME

That which makes a mother. The mother of all is Nature.
Her cradle is the Earth.

www.globalcommunity.org/flash/index.shtml
Two wonderful films about life on Earth. *The Wombat* is
about the interconnectedness of all life and will make you
chuckle, and *An Extraordinary Moment* tells our universal
story.

www.oneearth.org
Click on **communications**, then **campaigns**, and view
the films made for each year. Start with '95, a film called
Mother.

Y

YOUNG PEOPLE

www.abc.net.au/science/planetslayer/default.htm
Play these interactive games from Australia, and discover how your chosen lifestyle could affect the Earth. Click on **greenhouse calculator** and find out when you should die!

www.changetheworldkids.com
A group of twenty-one young people in the town of Woodstock, Vermont, where I live, started giving their services free to the community: baby-sitting, building clothes lines, helping seniors, repairing sub-standard housing. They then went on to an even bigger project: the Costa Rican rainforest. They have planted hundreds of trees to help save critical migratory-corridor habitats for songbirds, have started a tree nursery, and are working with the local coffee farmers to support their growing of Fairtrade coffee, which we can now buy in our local shops. They are a wonderful example of how young people can change the world with a big dream and simple steps.

www.ecomall.com/biz/kidslinks.htm
Links for kids about the world and how it works.

www.ecotimecapsule.com
In 2044, time capsules that were buried in Mexico, Britain, South Africa, the Seychelles and Australia fifty years previously, on World Environment Day in 1994, will be

opened, perhaps by those who were present at the burial ceremonies as children. In **time capsule** you can find out the contents of the capsule buried at Ness Botanical Gardens on the Wirral, and **where to now** has a list of **twenty-one ways to be green**. Print it out and pin it up where everyone can read it, at school and at home. Read the children's **poems** and **letters** that were included in the capsules, and click on **what's new** for the events of the ten-year anniversary in 2004.

www.envision.uk.net
'Envision gave me the confidence to make a difference and change the unchangeable.' *Vivianna, Envision team member, aged seventeen, Maria Fidelis School.*

Envision helps young people develop the skills, awareness and commitment they need to bring positive change for the better to their world.

www.futurescapes.com.au
An interactive website introducing you to a range of futures that are dependent upon your environmental choices.

www.ibuydifferent.org
This site for young people, created by the World Wildlife Fund and the Center for a New American Dream, highlights the importance of the consumer choices young people make, and how their inventive imaginations can really make a difference to their future.

www.idealist.org/kt/youthorgs.html
Environmental organizations started by kids. Follow in their footsteps and start your own.

www.naturedetectives.org.uk

Become a nature detective, and help gather important information about how climate change is affecting species habitat. **Identify** helps you name what you are looking at in the natural world, and then you can **record** it. There are pictures to colour in **resources**, and lots of material to download. **Discovery** has games, ideas for parents and teachers, and **overview** lists the resources in this packed website.

www.rspb.org.uk/youth/learn/index.asp

If you're doing a project about birds, or just curious about why their bills are shaped the way they are and what they eat, you will find great answers here. There are also games and jigsaws to enjoy in an idle moment.

www.wearev.com

V is a volunteer organization for sixteen to twenty-five-year-olds run by young people whose mission is to develop their contemporaries' talents, skills and self-confidence, while they have fun working to improve their communities and environment.

web.ukonline.co.uk/conker/pond-dip

This site, which is created by kids for kids, is all about wildlife ponds and the creatures that live in them. It tells you **how to make a wildlife pond**, what you need to start dipping into it, and what you might find. When something exciting turns up you can take a picture, write a report and post them on this site. And while you're at it, they also want your drawings.

www.yesworld.org

Youth for Environmental Sanity educates, inspires and empowers young people to live their ideals daily.

Z

ZERO POPULATION GROWTH

Overpopulation is the root cause of every environmental problem. The key to survival on our planet is population control. Support organizations that work humanely to bring net human-population growth to zero.

opr.princeton.edu/popclock
A world-population clock. Watching it count is a sobering experience.

www.populationaction.org/issues/index.htm
Population Action International lays out the problems that runaway population growth causes, including its impact on humanity's hopes for peace.

ACKNOWLEDGEMENTS

My thanks go to:
Sarah Emsley for being a wonderfully patient editor;
Maria Coughlin for the indexing;
Liz Ambros, without whom neither my life nor my computer
    would work;
Margo Baldwin of Chelsea Green Publishing for her vision
    and encouragement;
Roger Payne for providing a bureau of standards and love.

INDEX

Note: Entries in bold are major discussions.

Art 1

* Planet Under Pressure.
* Top Sites.
* Virunga National Park
* 7 problems
* Wetlands
* Social Ecology

* AvA
* Berk bits 2007
+
✗
➴